LLYFR TI A FI

A Handbook for parents, toddlers and babies who are learning Welsh

Anne Brooke

Arlunydd: Lin Jenkins

GWASG GOMER 1984

Argraffiad cyntaf—Gorffennaf 1984
Ail Argraffiad—1988
Trydydd Argraffiad—1992
Pedwerydd Argraffiad—Mawrth 1995

ISBN 0 86383 093 5

Ⓗ Anne Brooke Ⓒ

Cedwir pob hawl. Ni ellir atgynhyrchu unrhyw ran o'r cyhoeddiad hwn na'i gadw mewn
cyfundrefn adferadwy na'i drosglwyddo mewn unrhyw ddull na thrwy unrhyw gyfrwng,
electronig, electrostatig, tâp magnetig, mecanyddol, ffotogopïo, recordio, nac fel arall, heb
ganiatâd ymlaen llaw gan y cyhoeddwyr Gwasg Gomer, Llandysul, Dyfed.

Argraffwyd gan J. D. Lewis a'i Feibion Cyf., Gwasg Gomer, Llandysul, Dyfed

For Mother

INTRODUCTION

1. Purpose
To help parents of children in Welsh Mother and Toddler groups (children under 3) to teach and use Welsh at home and also in the weekly or twice-weekly meetings of the group.

2. Contents
a. Each basic activity is introduced on a single page.
On this page you will find the simple language that will enable you and your child to perform the activity in Welsh.

b. On the facing page you will find:
1) Variations on the sentence pattern and vocabulary for the activity.
2) Songs and games associated with the activity.
3) Other useful information.

c. In the back of the book are Further Hints for each activity.
These include:

1) For the ambitious parent—further variations on activities and sentence patterns.
2) Grammatical notes.
3) Vocabulary.
4) More useful information.

Each activity is essentially self-contained. The sequence suggested for each term is therefore by no means obligatory, and you may follow any order that seems best to you when introducing the activities to your child.

3. The Mabon Books
The 10 Mabon books suggested for reading have been especially designed for learner parents and very young children, although they will be enjoyed by older children as well.
They will enable:
a. Parents to read to their children in Welsh after a practice session of 5 minutes or less.
b. Children of 18 months or less to recognise basic sentence patterns and vocabulary.
c. Both parents and children to enjoy reading a story in Welsh together.

4. Final Comments
For the child under 3 almost everything that he experiences is new and exciting. He is as happy to help you lay the table and hang out the washing as to play a game of Hide and Seek or sing a song. All of these activities are learning activities in any language. When your child helps you to sort the laundry he is developing matching skills and a sense of size and colour; when he plays Hide and Seek he learns the meaning of "in" and "under" and "behind"; when he is singing and performing action songs he is not only enjoying himself and learning how to sing and move, but is developing such concepts as "up" and "down" and "fast" and "slow". The activities in this book have been chosen because they will help your child to develop generally, as well as because they are the easiest and most effective way to teach and learn Welsh.

Children learn how to talk almost from birth to 36 months. This is the **only** period in their lives during which it is as easy for them to learn two or more languages as it is for them to learn one. If you make the activities introduced in this book part of your normal everyday routine, your child will have a good knowledge of basic Welsh vocabulary and sentence patterns by the time that he enters nursery or infant school at the age of 3.

HOW TO USE THE HANDBOOK

1. Find a Welsh speaking teacher or choose the mother who knows the most Welsh to act as the leader of your group.

2. During each group session spend

   a. 10-15 minutes with your leader (and / or any other Welsh speaking mother)
      1) Practising the activity for the week ahead.
      2) Reviewing old songs and learning new ones.
      3) Practising reading the Mabon book for the week, if any.
      If your child wants to join you during this practice period, all the better.

   b. 10-15 minutes with the children singing songs (and concentrating on action songs at the beginning), playing games, and perhaps going over simple language routines (such as naming a few parts of the body).

   c. The rest of the time playing, talking, and having coffee and juice together.

   NOTE TO GROUP LEADER:
   It is **essential** that you go over the new activity, etc. each week with your mothers, no matter how noisy and disruptive the children may sometimes be.
   Only in this way will the majority of mothers acquire not only the necessary facility in pronunciation, but also the confidence and inspiration to try out particular situations at home from week to week.

3. At home

   a. Introduce one new activity each week.

   b. Once you have introduced a particular activity practise it **every** day or on any suitable occasion (depending on the nature of the activity).
   CHILDREN LEARN BEST THROUGH CONSTANT REPETITION IN ROUTINE SITUATIONS.

   c. Use as little English as possible even the first time that you introduce an activity. Your gestures and example are the best method of showing your child the meaning of the Welsh words. After the first time it should seldom, if ever, be necessary for you to use any English at all.

   d. Your goal is to build up a pattern of activities throughout the day in which you can use basic Welsh with your child (see Supplement 3).

   You are **not** expected to change the language of your household entirely to Welsh (although you may decide to do this at some future time).

   All that is required is that you take each routine situation of the day as it occurs (getting up, getting dressed, having breakfast, etc.) and use the few Welsh phrases thay you know for that situation. You may then go on to say everything else in English. The important thing is to **remember** to do this every day until the Welsh words and phrases become a habit for you and your child.

   NOTE TO PARENTS IN NORTH WALES
   North Wales vocabulary and sentence patterns, where they differ from those used in South Wales, are provided in Supplement 2. Remember to use them!

CONTENTS

WORK OF THE AUTUMN TERM

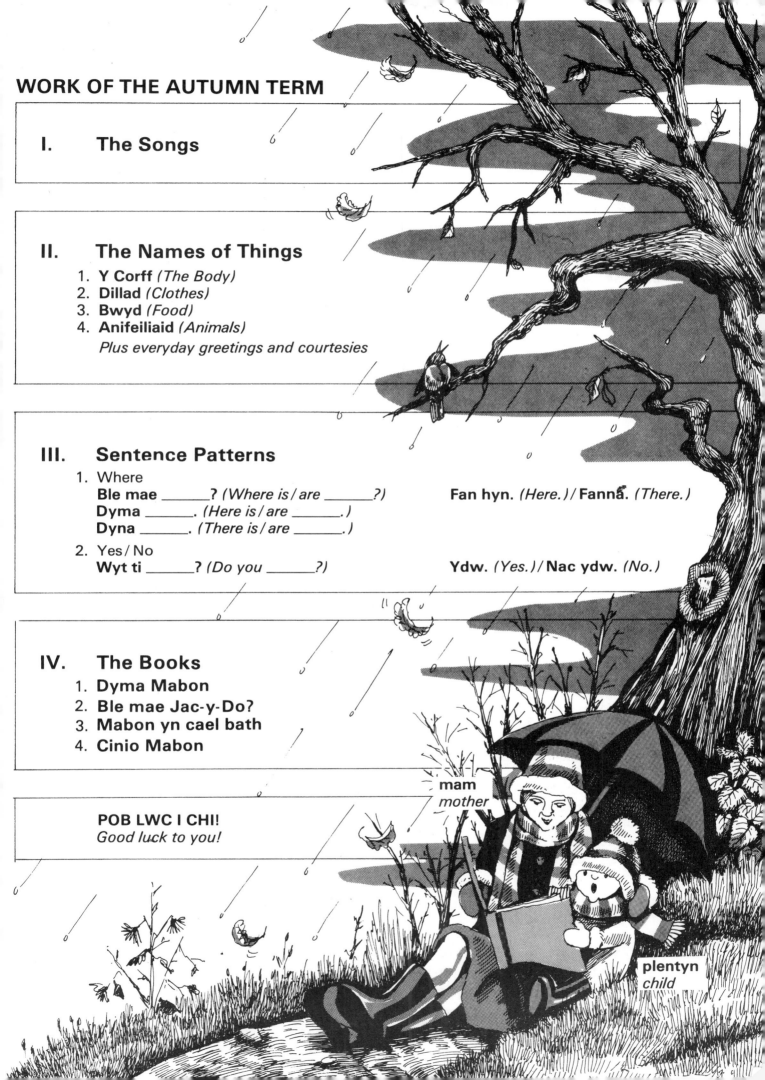

I.   The Songs

II.   The Names of Things
1. **Y Corff** *(The Body)*
2. **Dillad** *(Clothes)*
3. **Bwyd** *(Food)*
4. **Anifeiliaid** *(Animals)*

    Plus everyday greetings and courtesies

III.   Sentence Patterns
1. Where
   Ble mae _____? *(Where is / are _____?)*   **Fan hyn.** *(Here.)* / **Fanna.** *(There.)*
   Dyma _____. *(Here is / are _____.)*
   Dyna _____. *(There is / are _____.)*
2. Yes / No
   Wyt ti _____? *(Do you _____?)*   **Ydw.** *(Yes.)* / **Nac ydw.** *(No.)*

IV.   The Books
1. **Dyma Mabon**
2. **Ble mae Jac-y-Do?**
3. **Mabon yn cael bath**
4. **Cinio Mabon**

mam
mother

plentyn
child

POB LWC I CHI!
Good luck to you!

1
Y CANEUON
The Songs

SUT
How

1. Sing as many songs as you and the children have time and energy for every time that your group meets. Concentrate on action songs whenever possible and especially at the beginning.
2. Spend at least 5 or 10 minutes each day singing Welsh songs with your child at home.

y mamau (the mothers)
y plant (the children)
yr athrawes (the teacher)

Important: *Mothers should have learned these 10 songs by the end of the second week.*

1. (Hwiangerddi 1.3)
Un llaw i fyny,
Un llaw i lawr,
Dwy law i fyny,
Dwy law i lawr.

Un fraich i fyny,
Un fraich i lawr,
Dwy fraich i fyny,
Dwy fraich i lawr.

Un droed i fyny,
Un droed i lawr,
Dwy droed i fyny,
Dwy droed i lawr.

One hand up,
One hand down,
Two hands up,
Two hands down.

One arm up,
One arm down,
Two arms up,
Two arms down.

One foot up,
One foot down,
Two feet up,
Two feet down.

('Dawns y bysedd' from **Hwyl wrth Ganu**, Falyri Jenkins; see Useful Information, p.3)

2.
Ble mae bawdyn? Ble mae bawdyn?
Dyma fi. Dyma fi.
Sut mae heddiw? Da iawn, diolch.
I ffwrdd â ti, i ffwrdd â ti!

(Tune: Frère Jacques)

Where is thumbkin? Where is thumbkin?
Here I am. Here I am.
How are (things) today? Very good, thanks.
Away with you, away with you.

PAM
WHY

1. To enjoy singing in Welsh together.
2. To teach your child actions, the names of things, sentence patterns, counting, colours and other describing words—almost anythyng—in Welsh altogether painlessly.

Mi Welais Jac-y-Do (£1.75) (plus the accompanying **Handbook for Welsh Learner Parents** which includes translations, grammar, and a vocabulary of over 500 words (£1.50)) (both published by Gwasg Gomer, Llandysul) is a useful collection of old and new nursery rhymes and songs. The detailed illustrations make it easy for both parents and children to learn as they sing.

The songs in **Mi Welais Jac-y-Do** are included with others on two cassettes published by the Mudiad Ysgolion Meithrin (Welsh Nursery Schools Movement) — **Hwiangerddi** (£1) and **Hwyl wrth Ganu** (£4.85). If you are not familiar with the songs and their tunes and want to hear and practice them at home, you can send for the cassettes to Swyddfa Mudiad Ysgolion Meithrin, 10 Park Grove, Caerdydd, CF1 3BN. They are also available in most Welsh book shops.

The Actions

1.
Raise one hand, arm, etc. or two as required.

2.
Both hands behind you.
Bring out first one thumb and then the other.
Wiggle one thumb and then the other.
Put one thumb behind you and then the other.

Good Advice

Since not every one can afford to pay £4.85 for the cassette **Hwyl wrth Ganu,** buy a copy for your group so that you can learn new songs together whenever you meet.

Y Caneuon (parhad)
The Songs (continued)

3. (Hwiangerddi 1.7)
Troi ein dwylo, troi ein dwylo,
Troi a throi a throi fel hyn.

Curo'n dwylo, curo'n dwylo,
Clap a chlap a chlap fel hyn.

Chwifio'n dwylo, chwifio'n dwylo,
Chwifio, chwifio, lan fel hyn.

Twirl our hands, twirl our hands,
Twirl and twirl and twirl like this.

Clap our hands, clap our hands,
Clap and clap and clap like this.

Wave our hands, wave our hands,
Wave, wave, up like this.

4. (Hwyl wrth Ganu 2.2)
Un bys, dau fys, tri bys yn dawnsio,
Pedwar bys, pum bys, chwe bys yn
    dawnsio,
Saith bys, wyth bys, naw bys yn
    dawnsio,
Deg bys yn dawnsio'n llon.

One finger, two fingers, three fingers dancing,
Four fingers, five fingers, six fingers
    dancing,
Seven fingers, eight fingers, nine fingers
    dancing,
Ten fingers dancing merrily.

5. (Hwiangerddi 1.8)
Mynd ar y ceffyl, clipidi clop,
Mynd ar y ceffyl, drot drot drot;
Lan i'r mynydd, lawr i'r cwm,
Draw dros y dolydd, bwm bwm bwm.

Gyrru a gyrru, gyrru a gyrru,
Gyrru a gyrru fel y gwynt—O!

Going on the horse, clipity clop,
Going on the horse, trot trot trot;
Up to the mountain, down to the valley,
Yonder over the meadows, boom boom boom.

Ride and ride, ride and ride,
Ride and ride like the wind—Oh!

6. (Hwiangerddi 2.4)
Cysgu ar y llawr.
Cysgu ar y llawr.
Cau eich llygaid bach
A chysgu ar y llawr.

(Dihuno—Codi—Neidio!)

Sleep on the floor.
Sleep on the floor.
Close your little eyes
And sleep on the floor.

(Wake up—Get up—Jump!)

7. (Hwiangerddi 1.11)
'Nôl a 'mlaen. (8 times)

Lan a lawr. (8 times)

Troi a throi. (8 times)

Mewn a ma's. (8 times)

Backwards and forwards.

Up and down.

Turn and turn.

In and out.

3.

Twirl your hands around each other.

Clap hands together.

Wave hands up in the air.

4.

Starting with both fists closed, raise one finger at a time as you sing.

5.

Mother bounces child on her knee or rocks him on a rocking horse in time to the music.

6.

The children lie on the floor as their mothers sing. At the end, as she says "**Neidio!**", each mother lifts her child high into the air.

7.

Bend backwards and forwards.

Stand and sit (or squat).

Turn around first in one direction and then in the other.

Move hands in towards your chest and then out.

8.
Cylch o gylch rhosynnau
Poced llawn o flodau.
A-tish-w! A-tish-w!
I lawr â ni!

(Un-dau-tri-neidio!)

(The same tune as in English)

Ring-a-round-a-roses
A pocket full of flowers.
A-tish-oo! A-tish-oo!
Down with us!

(One-two-three-jump!)

9.
Hicori Dicori Doc (tic toc)
Llygoden lan y cloc (tic toc)
Mae'n taro tri
(Un-dau-tri)
I lawr â hi.
Hicori Dicori Doc.

(The same tune as in English)

Hickory Dickory Dock (tick tock)
A mouse up the clock (tick tock)
It's striking three
(One-two-three)
Down with her.
Hickory Dickory Dock.

Warning

You will not help your child to learn Welsh by simply turning on a cassette and then going about your business.

To show him the meaning of the Welsh words he hears you will need to:

1. Sing and perform action songs with him (with or without cassette)

and

2. In the case of non-action songs, turn to the relevant picture in **Mi Welais Jac-y-Do** and point to key objects as you sing.

8.
Walk around in a circle holding hands.
Fall down as you say "I lawr â ni!"
After counting to three, jump up again
as you say "Neidio!"

9.
Bend from side to side like a pendulum.
Lift hands up like the mouse.
Clap hands in time with "Un-dau-tri".
Fall down as you say "I lawr â hi".

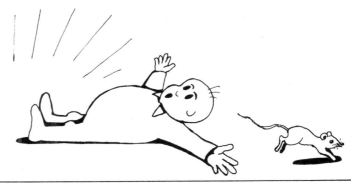

Y Caneuon (parhad)
The Songs (continued)

10. (Hwiangerddi 2.8)

Heno, heno, hen blant bach,	*Tonight, tonight, dear (old) little children,*
Heno, heno, hen blant bach,	*Tonight, tonight, dear (old) little children,*
Dime dime dime, hen blant bach,	*Ha'penny ha'penny ha'penny, dear . . .*
Dime dime dime, hen blant bach.	*Ha'penny ha'penny ha'penny, dear . . .*
Gwely, gwely, hen blant bach (2)	*Bed, bed, dear (old) little children*
Dime dime dime, hen blant bach. (2)	*Ha'penny ha'penny ha'penny, dear . . .*
'Fory, 'fory, hen blant bach (2)	*Tomorrow, tomorrow, dear (old) little children*
Dime dime dime, hen blant bach. (2)	*Ha'penny ha'penny ha'penny dear . . .*

Cerdded, cerdded yn y parc	*Walking, walking in the park*
Cerdded, cerdded yn y parc	*Walking, walking in the park*
Cerdded, cerdded, cerdded yn y parc	*Walking, walking, walking in the park*
Cerdded, cerdded, cerdded yn y parc.	*Walking, walking, walking in the park.*

Rhedeg, rhedeg lawr y bryn	*Running, running down the hill*
Rhedeg, rhedeg lawr y bryn	*Running, running down the hill*
Rhedeg, rhedeg, rhedeg lawr y bryn	*Running, running, running down the hill*
Rhedeg, rhedeg, rhedeg lawr y bryn.	*Running, running, running down the hill.*

Nofio, nofio yn y môr	*Swimming, swimming in the sea*
Nofio, nofio yn y môr	*Swimming, swimming in the sea*
Nofio, nofio, nofio yn y môr	*Swimming, swimming, swimming in the sea*
Nofio, nofio, nofio yn y môr.	*Swimming, swimming, swimming in the sea.*

Hedfan, hedfan yn yr awyr	*Flying, flying in the sky*
Hedfan, hedfan yn yr awyr	*Flying, flying in the sky*
Hedfan, hedfan, hedfan yn yr awyr	*Flying, flying, flying in the sky*
Hedfan, hedfan, hedfan yn yr awyr.	*Flying, flying, flying in the sky.*

Clapio dwylo un-dau-tri	*Clapping hands one-two-three*
Clapio dwylo un-dau-tri	*Clapping hands one-two-three*
Clapio, clapio, clapio un-dau-tri	*Clapping, clapping, clapping one-two-three*
Clapio, clapio, clapio un-dau-tri.	*Clapping, clapping, clapping one-two-three.*

Cysgu, cysgu yn y nos	*Sleeping, sleeping in the night*
Cysgu, cysgu yn y nos	*Sleeping, sleeping in the night*
Cysgu, cysgu, cysgu yn y nos	*Sleeping, sleeping, sleeping in the night*
Cysgu, cysgu, cysgu yn y nos.	*Sleeping, sleeping, sleeping in the night.*

The tune to this old traditional lullaby can be used to teach a number of action words as you walk, run, etc. in a circle and mime the various actions.

It is also a useful song with which to calm the children down at the end of a vigorous session.

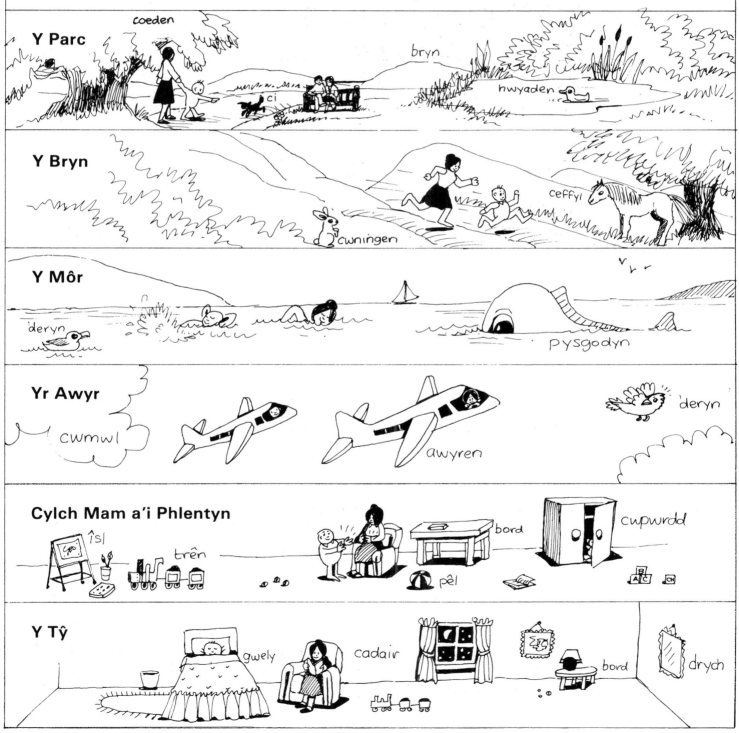

Y Parc
coeden
bryn
ci
hwyaden

Y Bryn
ceffyl
cwningen

Y Môr
'deryn
pysgodyn

Yr Awyr
cwmwl
awyren
'deryn

Cylch Mam a'i Phlentyn
îsl
trên
bord
cwpwrdd
pêl

Y Tŷ
gwely
cadair
bord
drych

2
TRWY'R DYDD
Through the Day

SUT
HOW

Repeat these phrases at appropriate moments
during the day.

Bore da.
Good morning.

Amser te.
Teatime.

Amser brecwast.
Breakfast time.

Amser gwely.
Bedtime.

Amser cinio.
Dinner time.

Nos da.
Good night.

PAM
WHY

To teach your child:
1. Everyday greetings in Welsh.
2. The Welsh words for mealtimes and bedtime. These are important because they are
   among the chief ways in which a small child marks time during her day.

You can also say:

	amser brecwast.
Mae'n	amser cinio.
It's	
	amser te.

1. Mae'n amser codi.
It's time to get up.

2. Mae'n amser brecwast.
It's breakfast time.

3. Mae'n amser cinio.
It's dinner time.

4. Mae'n amser te.
It's teatime.

5. Mae'n amser gwely.
It's bedtime.

6. Mae'n amser cysgu.
It's time to sleep.

Llongyfarchiadau!
Congratulations

1. You can now sing ten songs in Welsh and your child is beginning to know them too. There are over ninety different words in these songs. (Count them).
2. You can use eight separate Welsh phrases throughout the day and have a working vocabulary of at least ten words.

Here— as a bonus for your good work—
are the four most commonly used requests/commands in Welsh.

Dere 'ma.
Come here.

Cau'r drws.
Shut the door.

Ishte lawr.
Sit down.

Paid!
Don't!

Remember that it's never too soon to begin using Welsh with your baby.

3
CWRTEISI (etc.)
Courtesy

SUT
HOW

Repeat these phrases at appropriate moments during the day and encourage your child to do the same.

Diolch.
Thanks.

Diolch yn fawr.
Thanks a lot.

Dim diolch.
No thanks.

Dwed "Diolch".
Say "Thanks".

Os gweli di'n dda.
Please

Plîs.
Please.

(This may be used by children under 3 and by parents when in a hurry.)

Dwed "Plîs".
Say "Please".

PAM
WHY To teach your child:
Courtesy in Welsh.

IMPORTANT: How to praise your child in Welsh

Further Hints p.100

DA IAWN!
Very good! / Well done!

Bachgen da!
(Good boy!)

Merch dda!
(Good girl!)

Note: If your child is occasionally less than angelic, you would say:

 Bachgen drwg!
Bad boy!

 Merch ddrwg!
Bad girl!

Pobl *(People)*

Mami
menyw
(a woman)

Dadi
dyn
(a man)

merch fawr
(a big girl)

bachgen mawr
(a big boy)

merch fach
(a little girl)

y babi
(the baby)

bachgen
bach
(a little
boy)

SUT
HOW

Make a game out of naming parts of the body at bath time, when dressing and undressing your child, etc.

The game can also be played in the group when you gather together to sing songs.

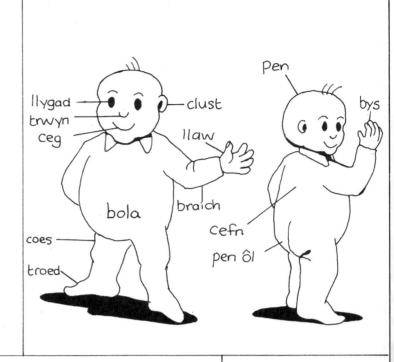

Ble mae
Where is

pen Mami?
Mammy's head?

pen Nia?

llaw Mami?
Mammy's hand?

llaw Dewi?

Fan hyn!
Here!

(touching the **pen**,
etc.)

PAM
WHY   To teach your child:
1.   The names of parts of the body in Welsh.
2.   The sentence pattern:

   Ble mae _____? *(Where is / are _____?)*   **Fan hyn!** *(Here!)*

3.   The Welsh way of showing possesson:

pen Mami	**llaw Nia**	**bys Dewi**
Mammy's head	*Nia's hand*	*Dewi's finger*

The easiest way to teach and learn parts of the body in Welsh is through action songs such as:

Ble mae bawdyn?
Un llaw i fyny
Troi ein dwylo
Un bys, dau fys

which you already know (pp. 2 and 4) and also:

Dyma'r ffordd i olchi wyneb *(see pp. 23 and 103)*

and

Dwy fraich ar led (*see* **Mi Welais Jac-y-Do)**

In the group your leader will say:

Ble mae eich
Where is your

braich?

bys?

coes?

troed?

Fan hyn!

More Useful Information

Llyfr yr Wythnos
Book of the Week

There is no word in Welsh for the English "a".

pen   **llaw**   **troed**
a head   *a hand*   *a foot*

Dyma Mabon

5
ANIFEILIAID Y FFERM
Animals of the Farm

SUT
HOW

Use the pictures on these pages to teach your child the names of animals and the sounds they make.

Then move on to the real thing with your pets or the animals you see as you go for a walk or a drive.

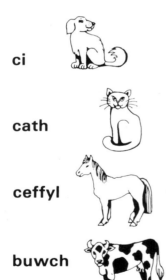

ci

cath

ceffyl

buwch

W-wff W-wff!

Miaw!

Neee!

Mw Mw!

PAM
WHY   To teach your child:
1. *The Welsh names of farm animals.*
2. *The sounds farm animals make.*
3. *The sentence patterns:*

Dyma _____ *(Here is / Here are* _____*)*
Ble mae'r _____**? Fan hyn!**   *(Where is the* _____*?   Here!)*

ddafad

Me Me!

mochyn

Rhoch Rhoch!

hwyaden

Cwac Cwac!

Dyma'r
(Here is the)

afr

Me Me!

iâr

Clwc Clwc!

ceiliog

Cocadwdldww!

Llyfr yr Wythnos
Book of the Week

Useful Information

Ble mae Jac-y-Do?

Y — *The*

y ceffyl   **y ci**
the horse   *the dog*

Some songs about animals are:

Mynd ar y ceffyl
Gee, geffyl bach
Dau gi bach
Fferm yr Hafod
Ceiliog coch

1.   *y becomes* **yr** *before vowels (a e i o u w y)*
and **h**.

yr afr   **yr hwyaden**
the goat   *the duck*

2.   **y** *becomes* **'r** *after vowels.*

Dyma'r ceffyl.   Ble mae'r hwyaden?

*(see **Mi welais Jac-y-Do**)*

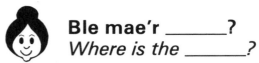

Ble mae'r _____?
Where is the _____?

mynydd

bryn

y cae

y beudy

buwch
Y fuwch

Cath,
Y gath

ceiliog

hwyaden

gafr
yr afr

dafad
Y ddafad

Do you know what?

You have completed half of the work of the term!

By now you and your child know:

1. At least 10 Welsh songs and the actions that go with them.

2. How to mark the time in Welsh.

3. How to be polite in Welsh (and also how to go to the toilet).

4. The Welsh names for many important parts of the body.

5. The Welsh names for farm animals and the noises they make.

You have also read two books in Welsh.
DA IAWN!

You are now ready for the next important step:
WASHING YOUR HANDS IN WELSH!

6
GOLCHI DWYLO
Washing Hands

Further Hints p.103

SUT
HOW

Use these Welsh phrases when you help your child to wash her hands.

PAM
WHY

To teach your child:
1. *To perform everyday actions in Welsh.*
2. *The pattern*

   Dyma _____ *(Here is / are* _____ *)*

3. *The command words*

Golcha	**Sycha**
Wash	*Dry*

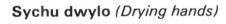

mwd

Golchi dwylo *(Washing hands)*	**Sychu dwylo** *(Drying hands)*
Mae'n amser golchi dwylo nawr.	**Mae'n amser sychu dwylo nawr.**
It's time to wash (your) hands now.	*It's time to dry (your) hands now.*
Dyma'r sebon.	**Dyma'r lliain.**
Here is the soap.	*Here's the towel.*
Golcha dy ddwylo.	**Sycha dy ddwylo.**
Wash your hands.	*Dry your hands.*

DA IAWN, CARIAD!

Cân Olchi Dwylo *(Hand Washing Song)*	**Llyfr yr Wythnos**
(Tune: "Here we go round the mulberry bush")	
1. **Dyma'r ffordd i olchi dwylo** *Here's the way to wash (your) hands*	**Mabon yn cael bath**
I olchi dwylo, i olchi dwylo;	
Dyma'r ffordd i olchi dwylo	
Yn gynnar yn y bore. *Early in the morning.*	
2. **Dyma'r ffordd i sychu dwylo (etc.)** *Here's the way to dry (your) hands*	

7
DILLAD
Clothes

SUT
HOW

Play this clothes game perhaps once or twice a day for a week—until your child can either point to all his clothes by their Welsh names or refuses to play any more.

Ble mae dy fest ?

Merch *(Girl)* | **Bachgen** *(Boy)*

Ble mae dy
Where is / are your

bants?   ffrog?

fest?   sanau?

bais?   sgidiau?

Ble mae dy
Where is / are your

bants?   drowsus?

fest?   sanau?

grys?   sgidiau?

   FAN HYN!

PAM
WHY   To teach your child:
1. The Welsh names for the clothes he wears every day.
2. The sentence pattern:

   Ble mae dy _____? *(Where is / are your _____?)*   **Fan hyn!** *(Here!)*

As you pull a shirt or dress or jumper over your child's head, say:

Ble mae Dewi?
Where is Dewi?

Dyma fe!
Here he is!

Ble mae Nia?
Where is Nia?

Dyma hi!
Here she is!

Once your child begins to join in himself he'll say:

Dyma fi !
Here I am!

Outdoor Clothes

Ble mae dy

siwmper?

gardigan?

got?

het?

Dyma dy

sgarff.

fenig.

welis.

ymbarêl.

Cân Wisgo/Dynnu Dillad *(A Dressing / Undressing Song)*

A song for those of you who feel lively early in the morning or late at night. It will help you and your child to learn an important new sentence pattern as well as the names of his clothes. *

Fel hyn 'wy'n gwisgo 'sgidiau *Like this I put on shoes*	**Fel hyn 'wy'n tynnu 'sanau** *Like this I take off socks*
'Sgidiau 'sgidiau	**'Sanau 'sanau**
Fel hyn 'wy'n gwisgo 'sgidiau	**Fel hyn 'wy'n tynnu 'sanau**
Yn y bore. *In the morning.*	**Yn y nos.** *In the night.*

*For the tune use "**Fel hyn mae mam yn golchi**" on the cheap (£1) cassette **Hwiangerddi**.

8
BWYD: AMSER BRECWAST
Food: Breakfast Time

SUT
HOW

As you serve breakfast to your child and other members of the family, make a habit of saying what the food is in Welsh.

Dyma'r.... sudd oren uwd creision ŷd tost menyn jam marmalêd mêl wy wedi ferwi wy wedi botsio wy wedi ffrio cig moch bara saim te coffi llaeth siwgr......

Dyma'r
Here is the

sudd oren.
orange juice.

tost.
toast.

menyn.
butter.

jam.
jam.

llaeth.
milk.

PAM
WHY   To teach your child:
1.   The Welsh names of the food she eats for breakfast every day.
2.   The sentence pattern:

Dyma _____   (*Here is / are* _____)

For most mothers the following 5 sentences will probably suffice:

Further Hints p.105

Dyma dy
Here is your

sudd oren.

sirial.
cereal.

dost.
toast

wy.
egg.

laeth.

Diolch yn fawr!

Ych -a-fi! (Ugh!)

Bwyd Brecwast

Sudd Oren

jwg / glas / oren

Uwd
Porridge

basn siwgr / llaeth / uwd

Creision Ŷd
Cornflakes

Creision ŷd / dysgl / llwy

Tost

tost / mâl / menyn

Wy

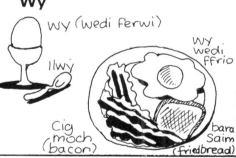

wy (wedi ferwi) / llwy / wy wedi ffrio / Cig moch (bacon) / bara saim (fried bread)

Llaeth/ Coffi/ Te

llaeth / te / coffi heb siwgr. (coffee without sugar.)

Cân Amser Brecwast *(A Breakfast Time Song)*

If you and your child are feeling exceptionally ambitious one morning, you can learn the Welsh for whatever she's eating and drinking that day by singing (to the tune of "The farmer wants a wife"):

Fel hyn 'wy'n b'yta tost.
Like this I eat toast.

Fel hyn 'wy'n b'yta tost.

Hei ho di hei di ho

Fel hyn 'wy'n b'yta tost.

Fel hyn 'wy'n yfed llaeth.
Like this I drink milk.

Fel hyn 'wy'n yfed llaeth.

Hei ho di hei di ho

Fel hyn 'wy'n yfed llaeth.

Between Breakfast and Dinner: An Artistic Interlude

SUT
HOW

Whenever your child paints, colours, pastes, or plays with dough, name the materials, colours (see p. 94), etc. in Welsh as you hand them to him.

Y Llun

Dyma'r
Here's the

îsl.

ffedog.

papur.

brws.

paent.

Dyma'r
Here's the

toes.
dough.

creon
glas etc.

creonau.

past.

siswrn.

Wyt ti eisiau
Do you want

peintio?
to paint?

tynnu llun?
to draw a picture?

gwneud rhywbeth?
to make something?

Ydw. / Na.
Yes. / No.

PAM
WHY

1. To give your child the "learning experience" — and fun — of working with paint, paste, dough, etc.
2. To teach your child:

    The names of art materials and colours in Welsh.

Useful Information: **THINGS TO MAKE IN WELSH:**	*(Most of these ideas were contributed by Marion Maw, Swyddog Datblygu Morgannwg Ganol / Development Officer Mid Glamorgan)*

Here are some easy things to make from toilet rolls, egg cartons, and pipe cleaners. You do the cutting, but encourage your child to do the painting and the pasting. Be sure that you both learn the Welsh word for the thing you make.

1. Blodyn *(Flower)*

1. 1 cup from the bottom of an egg carton.
2. 1 pipe cleaner for the **coes** (stem).
3. **Paent.** (Paint).

2. Corryn *(Spider)*

1. 1 cup from the bottom of an egg carton.
2. Pipe cleaners for the **coesau** (legs) and a handle.
3. **Paent** for the **corff** (body) and **llygaid** (eyes).

3. Siani Flewog *(Caterpillar)*

1. 3 cups from the bottom of an egg carton.
2. Pipe cleaners for feelers.
3. **Paent i'r corff a'r llygaid.** (Paint for the body and the eyes).

4. Malwoden *(Snail)*

1. 3 cups from the bottom of an egg carton, one pasted on top to make the **cragen** (shell).
2. Pipe cleaners for the **cyrn** (horns).
3. **Paent.**
4. **Past.**

5. Cyw Bach ac Wy *(Chick and Egg)*

1. 1 cup from the bottom of an egg carton for the **wy.**
2. Cotton wool (coloured) for the **cyw bach.**
3. **Papur** for the **pig** (beak). Also **past.**
4. **Paent** for the **llygaid.**

6. Plismon *(Policeman)* / Dyn Tân *(Fireman)*

1. 1 toilet roll for the **corff** and 1 cup from the bottom of an egg carton for the helmet.
2. **Papur i'r traed** (feet).
3. **Paent glas neu goch** (blue or red) **a du** (black).
4. **Past.**

7. Menyw *(Woman)*

1. 1 toilet roll for the **corff** and 1 cup from the bottom of an egg carton for the **het** (hat) /**gwallt** (hair).
2. **Papur i'r traed a'r ffedog** (apron).
3. **Paent.**
4. **Past.**

9

BWYD: AMSER CINIO
Food: Dinner Time

SUT
HOW

Play this food game as you serve dinner (etc.)
to your child and to other members of the
family.

Ble mae'r
Where is / are the

cawl?
soup?

bara menyn?
bread and butter?

sosej?

sglodion?
chips?

afal?
apple?

Fan hyn!
Here!

PAM
WHY   To teach your child:
1.   The Welsh names of the food he eats for dinner every day.
2.   The sentence pattern:

   Ble mae _____? *(Where is / are _____?)*   **Fan hyn!** *(Here!)*

A typical dinner time sequence might go like this:

Ble mae'r

bastai?
pie?

sglodion?

banana?

creision?
crisps?

llaeth?

Fan hyn!

Bwyd Cinio

Cawl 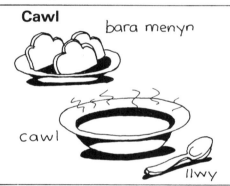	**Sosej/Ffa Coch/Wy** *Baked Beans*  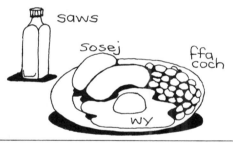	**Brechdanau** *Sandwiches* 
Pysgod a Sglodion *Fish and Chips* 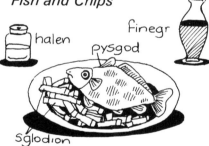	**Ffrwythau** *Fruit* 	**Bisgedi a Losin** *Biscuits and Sweets* 

Cawl: bara menyn, cawl, llwy

Sosej/Ffa Coch/Wy: saws, sosej, ffa coch, wy

Brechdanau: caws, brechdan gaws, brechdan jam

Pysgod a Sglodion: halen, finegr, pysgod, sglodion

Ffrwythau: afal, oren, banana

Bisgedi a Losin: bisgien, bisgedi, bisgedi siocled (chocolate), losin

Cân Amser Cinio *(A Dinner Time Song)*

Not quite so much energy is required to sing this dinner time song:

Fel hyn 'wy'n b'yta wy.
Like this I eat an egg.

Fel hyn 'wy'n b'yta wy.

Hei ho di hei di ho

Fel hyn 'wy'n b'yta wy.

Useful Information

At the end of a meal most children like to say in a singsong voice:

We-di gorff-en!

Which means "Fi-nished!"

Wedi gorff-en!

31

10
BWYD: AMSER TE
Food: Teatime

SUT
HOW

As you offer your child food, ask her in Welsh whether she wants particular things (starting with the ones she likes best).

At the beginning she will probably only nod or shake her head, but from 2½ on you may expect her to anser **Ydw** *(Yes)* or **Na** *(No)*.

Beth'wyt ti eisiau i ginio?

Sglodion, losin, bisgedi, pop, creision, losin, siocled, hufen iâ, losin, pwdin reis, losin.......

bisgïen?
a biscuit?

pop?

Wyt ti eisiau*
Do you want

losin?
sweets?

Ydw./Na.
Yes. / No.
or
Nac ydw.**

creision?
crisps?

hufen iâ?
ice cream?

*Pronounced **ee-sheh** *in S. Wales:* **ee-sho** *in N. Wales.*
** Pronounced **Nag** *ydw.*

PAM
WHY

To teach your child:
1. The Welsh names of the food she eats for tea every day.
2. The sentence pattern:

Wyt ti _____?	**Ydw./Na. (Nac ydw.)**
Do you _____?	*Yes. / No.*

Some things your child might want at teatime.

Wyt ti eisiau

grefi?

halen?
salt?

salad?

llwy?
a spoon?

rhagor?
more?

Ydw./Na.

Bwyd Te/Swper

Cig/Pys/Tatws
Meat / Peas / Potatoes

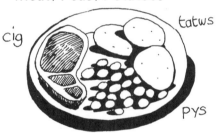

cig · tatws · pys

Ffowlyn/Grefi
Chicken / Gravy

cyllell · grefi · ffowlyn · fforc

Llysiau
Vegetables

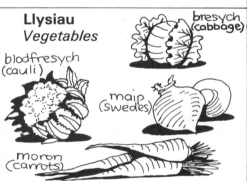

bresych (cabbage) · blodfresych (cauli) · maip (swedes) · moron (carrots)

Salad

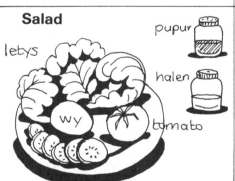

letys · pupur · halen · wy · tymato

Teisennau
Cakes

teisennau · teisen jam (jam cake)

Pwdin

pwdin reis (rice pudding) · hufen iâ (ice cream)

Cân Amser Te *(A Teatime Song)*

By teatime you'll be ready to sing with enthusiasm:

Fel hyn 'wy'n b'yta pys.
Like this I eat peas.

Fel hyn 'wy'n b'yta pys.

Hei ho di hei di ho

Fel hyn 'wy'n b'yta pys.

Llyfr yr Wythnos

Cinio Mabon

SUT
HOW

1. Encourage the children to sit together around a table to have their milk or squash and biscuits.
2. Speak only Welsh to the children at this time.

Ishte lawr *Sit down*	**fan hyn.** *here.* **wrth y ford.** *at the table.*		
Wyt ti eisiau *Do you want*	**bisgïen?** *a biscuit?* **bisgïen arall?** *another biscuit?* **llaeth?/squash?** *milk?/squash?* **rhagor o laeth?/ rhagor o squash?** *more milk?/squash?*	 **Ydw./Na.** *Yes./No.*	
Dwed *Say* **Wedi gorffen?** *Finished?*	**"Diolch".** *"Thanks".* **"Plîs".** **"Ydw"./"Nac ydw".**	**Diolch.** **Plîs.** **Ydw./Nac ydw.** **Wedi gorffen!** *Finished!*	

DA IAWN! *(Very good!)*

PAM
Why A. To teach the children:
   1. How to eat and drink in Welsh in a group situation.
   2. Courtesy in Welsh.
  B. To make the group sessions as Welsh as possible.

By now your morning should go something like this:

1. Mae'n amser codi.

2. Mae'n amser gwisgo.

3. Mae'n amser brecwast.

4. Mae'n amser canu *(to sing).*

5. Mae'n amser mynd i siopa *(to go to shop).*

6. Mae'n amser golchi dwylo nawr.

7. Mae'n amser cinio.

8. Mae'n amser cysgu!

WORK OF THE SPRING TERM

I.   The Names of Things
1. **Y Corff** *(The Body—more parts)*
2. **Celfi** *(Furniture)*
3. **Y Tŷ** *(The House)*
4. **Yr Ardd** *(The Garden)*
5. **Teganau** *(Toys)*

II.   Sentence Patterns
1. What
   Beth yw hwn? *(What is this?)*
   Beth yw'r rhain? *(What are these?)*

2. Doing Things
   Rho _____ **ar/yn/dan/wrth/tu ôl i** _____. *(Put* _____ *on / in / under / by / behind* _____*)*
   Cer i ôl _____. *(Go to fetch* _____*.)*

3. Yes / No
   Ydy e/hi _____**?** *(Is he / she* _____*?)*   **Ydy.** *(Yes.)* / **Nac ydy.** *(No.)*

III.   The Books
5. **Mabon yn peintio llun**
6. **Bwrw glaw**
7. **Ble mae Mabon?**

SUT
HOW

Make a game out of naming these additional parts of the body at bath time, when dressing or undressing your child, etc.

Remember that this is an excellent game to play in the group when you gather together to sing songs.

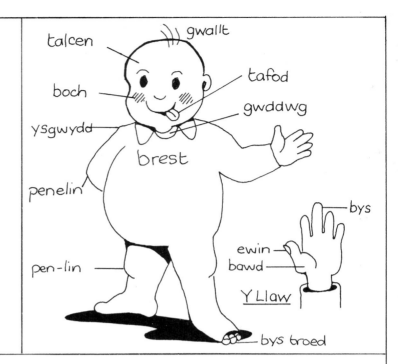

Ble mae
Where is

gwallt Mami?
Mammy's hair?

gwallt Nia?

tafod Mami?
Mammy's tongue

tafod Dewi?

Fan hyn!
Here!
(touching the
gwallt, *etc.)*

PAM
WHY *To teach your child:*

1. *The names of other parts of the body in Welsh.*
2. *The sentence pattern:*

   Ble mae _____? *(Where is / are _____?)*   **Fan hyn!**

3. *The Welsh way of showing possession:*

   gwallt Mami   **tafod Dewi**
   Mammy's hair   *Dewi's tongue*

Here is a good way to introduce the new body words during the group sessions. The children will learn quickly as they observe their mothers' movements and those of the group leader.

eich gwallt.

eich boch.

Rhowch eich bys ar
Put your finger on

eich ysgwydd.

eich brest.

eich pen-lin.

---

1. *If she wants you to go through the sequence again your leader will say:*

Eto.   **Unwaith eto.**
Again.   *Once again.*

2. *At the end your leader will surely say:*

DA IAWN!   **DA IAWN, WIR!**
Very good! /   *Very good, indeed!*
Well done!

Cân y Corff *(A Song of the Body)*

Here is a new song to sing on days when you are feeling particularly energetic. Put both hands on the appropriate parts of the body as you name them. (Tune: "There is a tavern in the town").

Pen ysgwyddau pen-lin traed
Head shoulders knee feet   } *(2)*

Pen-lin traed.

Pen ysgwyddau pen-lin traed. *(2)*

SUT
HOW

Whenever your child has a bath, name the things that he uses or plays with as you give them to him.

Dyma'r
Here is the

dŵr.
water.

sebon.
soap.

sbwng.
sponge.

clwtyn.
facecloth.

lliain.
towel.

PAM
WHY To teach your child:
1. *The Welsh names of things he uses in the bath.*
2. *The sentence pattern:*

   Dyma _____. *(Here is / Here are _____.)*

pysgodyn

cwch

hwyaden

glás

**potel,
y botel**

swigod

siampŵ

**brws
dannedd**

**past
dannedd**

Y 'Stafell 'Molchi *(The Bathroom)*

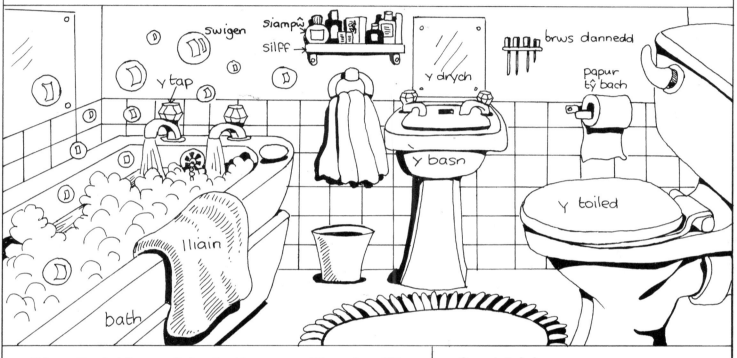

Cân y Bath *(Song of the Bath)* — see p. 23 and p. 103

Dyma'r ffordd i olchi braich (etc.) . . .
Here's the way to wash (your) arm . . .

*This song is probably the easiest and
pleasantest way of all to learn Welsh names
for parts of the body.*

Good Advice

This is an excellent moment to re-read

Mabon yn cael bath

More Good Advice:

*Every time that you fish for the soap or the facecloth in the tub or reach for a
towel or a toothbrush, remember to say:*

Ble mae'r

sebon?

clwtyn?

lliain?

brws dannedd?

Fan hyn!

Llongyfarchiadau!
Congratulations

By now you have taught your child:

1. To enjoy singing Welsh songs with you.
2. To enjoy listening to a story in Welsh.
3. To recognize the Welsh names for:
   a. The most important parts of the body.
   b. The clothes he wears every day.
   c. Farm animals.
   d. The food he eats every day.
   e. Things in the bath.
   and to point them when you ask the question:

   Ble mae _____?

The next important step is for him to name them himself when you ask:

Beth yw hwn?
What is this?

The easiest and most natural time to ask this question is when you are looking at a book together.

For further details turn to the next page.

SUT
HOW

Step 1

*As you read a story or look at a magazine or catalogue with your child, ask her in Welsh to show you where things are. Then **both** of you point to the person or object in question and say "**Fan hyn!**" ("Here!") or "**Fanna!**" ("There!").*

Ble mae Jac-y-do?

Step 1

Jac-y-Do?
Jackdaw?

ceffyl?
a horse?

Ble mae
Where is / are

'r bws?
the bus?

Fan hyn!
Here!

Fanna!
There!

het Jac-y-Do?
Jackdaw's hat?

Mami a Dadi Arth?
Mammy and Daddy Bear?

PAM *To enjoy looking at books with your child and to teach her to enjoy it too.*
WHY *To teach your child:*
1. The names of things in Welsh.
2. The sentence patterns:

Ble mae _____? *(Where is / are _____?)*
Beth yw hwn/hwnna? *(What is this / that?)*
Pwy yw hwn/hon? *(Who is this?)*

44

*Once again **you** ask the question but **both** of you give the answer.*

Beth yw hwn?
What is this?

Tŷ.
A house.

Ceffyl.
A horse.

Het.
A hat.

Note:

*For the learner parent the easiest books to begin on are **Mi Welais Jac-y-Do** (Welsh nursery rhymes and songs) plus accompanying **Handbook for Welsh Learner Parents** (Gwasg Gomer / Gomer Press) and some of the Gwasg y Dref Wen books (the Richard Scarry series, **Y Geiriadur Lliwgar (Welsh Children's Picture Dictionary)** etc.) In these books the pictures are entertaining and the Welsh words that you need ready to hand.*

Pwy yw hwn?
Who is this?—
male

Dadi Arth.
Daddy Bear.

Babi Arth.
Baby Bear.

Pwy yw hon?
Who is this?—
female

Mami Arth.
Mammy Bear.

Elen Benfelen.
Goldilocks.

Important Warning	**Llyfr yr Wythnos**
Most small children like to identify and point to people and things in books and magazines. But it is a temptation for the enthusiastic parent to overdo her questions and turn what should be fun (singing nursery rhymes, reading a story, looking at pictures) into a lesson and a chore. **Resist This Temptation!**	**Mabon yn peintio llun** 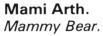

A Sample Singing Session (and don't forget to sing the song)

Step 1

Ble mae Jac-y-Do?

Ble mae Mami?

Ble mae'r sebon?

Ble mae'r hosan?

Fel hyn mae mam yn golchi,
Golchi, golchi;
Fel hyn mae mam yn golchi
Yn y tŷ.

ffedog

trowsus

Fel hyn mae mam yn smwddio,
Smwddio, smwddio;
Fel hyn mae mam yn swmddio
Yn y tŷ.

siten

Pwy yw hwn?

Pwy yw hon?

Beth yw hwn?

Beth yw hwnna?

SUT
HOW

When you put the wash
1. *Into the machine or dryer*
2. *Into the clothes basket after washing*
3. *Onto the clothesline*
4. *Into piles when sorting*
name some of the clothes (etc.) and their owners to your child in Welsh.

Sgert Mami.

Hosan Dadi.

Siwmper Nia.

Crys Dewi.

Blows Mam-gu.

Trowsus Tad-cu.

PAM
WHY   *To teach your child:*
1. *The Welsh names for clothes he and other members of the family wear every day.*
2. *The Welsh names for other things in the wash (sheets, blankets, etc.)*
3. *The Welsh way of showing possession.*

        sgert Mami   **hosan Dadi**
        Mammy's skirt   *Daddy's sock*

As you sort the laundry you can ask your child:

Ble mae
Where is

fest Dadi?

dy fest di?
your *vest?*

pais Mami?

dy bais di?
your *petticoat?*

hosan Mam-gu?

dy hosan di?
your *sock?*

Fan hyn!
Here!

Fanna!
There!

Y Teulu *(The Family)*

15

CELFI: Y 'STAFELL WELY
Furniture: The Bedroom

SUT
HOW

In this game you ask your child to point out to you the furniture, etc. in her bedroom. If she can already talk encourage her to take **her** turn asking the questions.

It shouldn't be necessary to play the game for more than a week.

Ble mae'r
Where is the

gwely?

gadair?

cwpwrdd?

ford?

drws?

Fan hyn!
Here!

Fanna!
There!

PAM
WHY To teach your child:
1. The Welsh names for the furniture, etc. in her bedroom.
2. The sentence pattern:

Ble mae _____? *(Where is / are _____?)*   **Fan hyn!/Fanna!** *(Here! / There!)*

Another Version

The furniture game can be conveniently played when you are looking at a catalogue or house and gardens magazine with your child too. Or you can use the picture above. Make a point of doing this once or twice during this week.

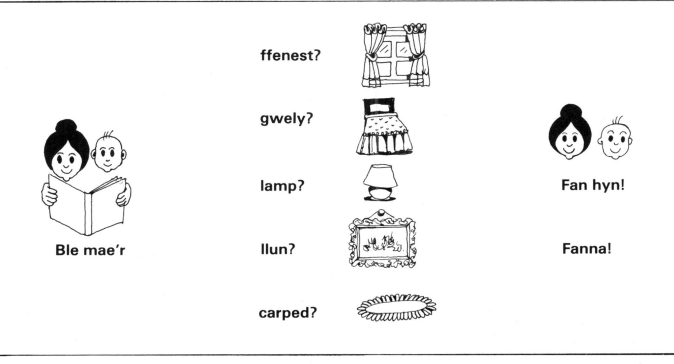

Ble mae'r

ffenest?

gwely?

lamp?

llun?

carped?

Fan hyn!

Fanna!

Y 'STAFELL FEITHRIN

pêl

| 1 | 2 | 3 |

cwpwrdd

tedi

Mistar Urdd

ffenest

llun

llenni

drws

ceffyl pren

llyfrau

dol

silff

blociau

A B C CH

carped

llithren

blodau

piano

llygoden

llyfr

bord

cadair

stôl

52

A Suggestion

You may want to introduce the furniture (etc.) finding game during one of your group meetings. In that case it can become a toy finding game too (see p. 57 for the Welsh names of toys). Mother and child operate as a unit and take turns asking the questions and finding the objects.

Alternatively — and with less effort — you can simply look at the picture on the opposite page with your child.

ceffyl?

piano?

llithren?

Ble mae'r

Fan hyn!

bêl?

llyfr?

cwpwrdd?

16
DILLAD: TYNNU DILLAD
Clothes: Undressing

SUT
HOW

As you help your child to undress ask him to put his clothes wherever you normally keep them.

Rho'r siwmper
Put the jumper

ar y gadair.
on

yn y fasged.
in

yn y drôr.
in

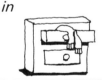

Rho'r 'sgidiau
Put the shoes

yn y cwpwrdd.
in

wrth y gadair.
by

dan y gadair.
under

Diolch yn fawr.
Thanks a lot.

Da iawn.
Very good.

PAM
WHY   To teach your child:
1.   The Welsh names of the clothes he wears every day.
2.   The Welsh names of the places to put his clothes.
3.   The Welsh place words (prepositions):

yn	**ar**	**wrth**	**dan**
in	*on*	*by*	*under*

4.   The sentence pattern:

Rho _____. *(Put _____.)*

Rho'r
Give the

ffrog

gardigan

i Mami, os gweli di'n dda.
to Mammy, please.

Rho'r
Give the

crys

trowsus

i fi, plîs.
to me, please.

Useful Information: *In many parts of South Wales* **doda** *(put) is commonly used instead of* **rho**.

Doda'r welis
Put the

yn y cwpwrdd.

wrth y drws.

dan y ford.

Doda'r 'sanau
Put the

wrth dy 'sgidiau.

yn y fasged.

ar y gwely.

A Suggestion	Llyfr yr Wythnos
If your child doesn't respond to your request at the beginning, then show him how it's done and say: **Fel hyn!** *Like this!*	**Bwrw glaw**

17
TEGANAU: TACLUSO
Toys: Tidying Up

SUT
HOW

As you and your child pick up her toys together ask her:

1. *To put one or two of them into a box or plastic washing-up bowl (12 months +).*
2. *To put one or more toys where they belong (slightly older children).*

1

Rho'r bêl
Put the ball

yn y bocs,
in the box,

yn y badell,
in the washing-up bowl,

os gweli di'n dda.
please.

2

Rho tedi
Put teddy

ar y gadair
on the chair

ar y gwely
on the bed

yn y cwpwrdd
in the cupboard

nawr.
now.

PAM
WHY *To teach your child:*

1. *The Welsh names of her toys.*
2. *The Welsh names of places to put her toys.*
3. *The Welsh place words (prepositions):*

ar	**yn**	**wrth**	**dan**
on	*in*	*by*	*under*

4. *The sentence pattern:*

   Rho _____. (Put _____.)

Teganau *(Toys)*

Further Hints p.114

pêl

dol

tedi

tŷ dol

car

trên

lori

ambiwlans

llestri te

llyfr

blociau

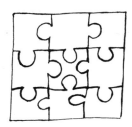

jig-so

awyren

beic

ceffyl pren

whilber

Some Further Practice

Rho'r

llyfr

blociau

jig-so

ar y silff.

Rho'r

ceffyl

beic

wrth y drws.

A Useful Phrase

Coda fe!—*Pick it up!*

57

More Bonus Phrases

Here are some things you have probably been wanting to say recently without knowing how.

Beth sy'n bod? *(What's the matter?)*

Mae'n flin 'da fi. *(I'm sorry.)*

mynydd

simnai

mwg

to

bryn

ffenest

coeden

sil

drws

blodau

lawnt

llwybr

perth

clwyd

wal

18
TEGANAU: CHWARAE
Toys: Playing

SUT
HOW

When you and your child want to play with a
particular toy, ask him to go and fetch it in
Welsh.

Cer i ôl tedi nawr.
Mae e lan llofft, yn
y bocs, ar y llawr, dan
y gwely, wrth y wal,
yn dy 'stafell di.

Cer i ôl tedi nawr.*
Go to fetch teddy now.

Mae e
He is

yn y parlwr.
in the parlour.

yn y gegin.
in the kitchen.

yn yr ardd.
in the garden.

lan llofft.
upstairs.

yn dy 'stafell di.
in your room.

*N. Wales—**Dos i ôl tedi rŵan.**

PAM
WHY To teach your child:
1. The Welsh names of his toys.
2. The Welsh names of the rooms / furniture in your house.
3. The Welsh place words (prepositions):

ar	**yn**	**wrth**	**dan**
on	*in*	*by*	*under*

4. The sentence patterns:

Cer i ôl _____. *(Go to fetch* _____. *) /***Dos i ôl** _____. *(Go to fetch* _____. *) (N. Wales)*
Mae e /hi _____. *(He / she (it) is* _____.*)*

Lan Llofft *(Upstairs)*

Lawr Llawr *(Downstairs)*

A Preliminary Step:

To teach your child the names of rooms in the first place, try this proven method. Taking him by the hand, go from one room to the other in your house while saying:

Rydyn ni'n mynd i
We are going to

'r gegin.		'r gegin.
'r parlwr.		'r parlwr.
'r 'stafell fyw.		**Dyma** 'r 'stafell fyw.
'r 'stafell 'molchi.		'r 'stafell 'molchi.
dy 'stafell wely (di).		dy 'stafell wely (di).

19

GÊM: CUDDIO 1 (Plentyn yn cuddio)
Game: Hide and Seek 1 (Child hiding)

SUT
HOW *Notice that the parent does most of the talking in* **Cuddio 1.**

Ble mae Nia?
Where is Nia

Ydy hi dan y soffa?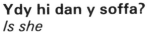
Is she

Nac ydy! *(pronounced*
(No!)   **Nag** *ydy)*

Ydy hi ar y piano?

Nac ydy!

Ydy hi tu ôl i'r drws?

Nac ydy!

Ydy hi tu ôl i'r gadair?

Ydy!   **Dyma hi!**
Yes!   *Here she is!*

PAM
WHY   *To have fun with your child in Welsh.*
To teach your child:
1.   *The Welsh names of the rooms / furniture in your house.*
2.   *The Welsh place words (prepositions)*

ar	yn	wrth	dan	tu ôl i
on	*in*	*by*	*under*	*behind*

3.   *The patterns*

Ble mae _____? *(Where is _____?)*
Ydy e /hi _____? Ydy./Nac ydy. *(Is he / she _____? Yes. / No.)*
Dyma fe! /hi! *(Here he / she is!)* / **Dyma fi!** *(Here I am!)*

If your child is a boy, you say:

Ble mae Dewi?

Ydy e dan y teledu?
Is he

Nac ydy.

Ydy e ar y silff ben tân?

Nac ydy.

Ydy e tu ôl i'r llenni?

Ydy! Dyma fe!
Yes! Here he is!

 Dyma fi! Here I am!

Y 'Stafell Fyw *(The Living Room)*

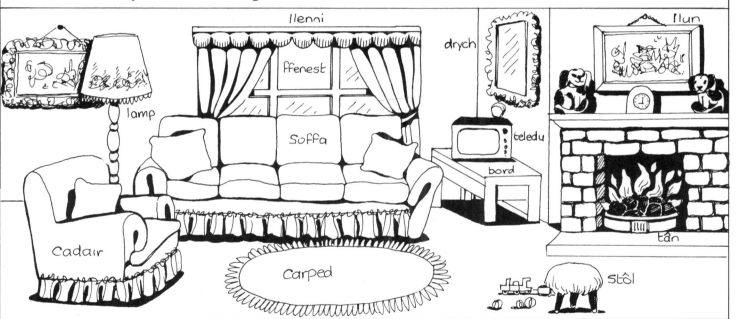

llenni

drych

llun

ffenest

lamp

Soffa

teledu

bord

Cadair

Carped

tân

Stôl

Here is a useful game / teaching song which can be played / sung in your group meetings and at home too (to the tune of "Frère Jacques").	**Llyfr yr Wythnos**

 Ble mae Nia? Ble mae Nia?

 Dyma fi. Dyma fi.
Here I am. Here I am.

 Dan y soffa. Dan y soffa.

 Dyma fi. Dyma fi.
Here I am. Here I am.

 Ble mae Dewi? Ble mae Dewi?

 Dyma fi. Dyma fi.
Here I am. Here I am.

 Ar y gadair. Ar y gadair.

 Dyma fi. Dyma fi.
Here I am. Here I am.

Ble mae Mabon?

63

20

GÊM: CUDDIO 2 (tedi/dol/etc. yn cuddio)
Game: Hide and Seek 2 (teddy/doll/etc. hiding)

SUT
HOW

*The parent or the child hides teddy (etc.) and then the child or the parent searches for him. Notice that the child needs to use more Welsh in **Cuddio 2** than in **Cuddio 1**.*

Ble mae tedi?
Where is teddy?

Ydy e wrth y blodyn?
Is he

Nac ydy! *(pronounced*
No! **Nag** *ydy)*

Ydy e yn y gwair?

Nac ydy!

Ydy e yn y cwt?

Nac ydy!

Ydy e tu ôl i'r goeden?

Ydy! Dyma fe!
Yes! Here he is!

PAM

WHY *To have fun with your child in Welsh.*
To teach your child:
1. *The Welsh names of places and things in the garden.*
2. *The Welsh place words (propositions)*

ar	yn	wrth	dan	tu ôl i
on	*in*	*by*	*under*	*behind*

3. *The patterns:*

Ble mae _____? *(Where is _____?)*
Ydy e/hi _____? Ydy./Nac ydy. *(Is he/she _____? Yes./No.)*
Dyma fe!/Dyma hi! *(Here he is!/Here she is!)*

Yr Ardd (The Garden)

Further Hints p.117

Cân yr Ardd (Song of the Garden)

"Sut mae plannu tatws?"

The words can be found in **Mi Welais Jac-y-Do** *(no. 13). the tune is the same as that for "Fel hyn mae mam yn golchi".*

If you are lucky enough to have a seesaw or a swing in your garden, you might want to repeat this traditional rhyme as your child moves up and down. Alternatively the rhyme is equally effective when you are simply jiggling your child on your knee.

Si-so Jac-y-Do
Seesaw Jackdaw

Dal y 'deryn dan y to.
Catch the bird under the roof.

Mynd i Lundain i roi tro
Go to London to pay a visit.

A dyna ddiwedd Jac-y-Do.
And there's an end of Jackdaw.

What can you and your child do in Welsh by now?

Wyt ti'n gallu
Can you

Canu yn Gymraeg?

Darllen yn Gymraeg?

Gwisgo yn Gymraeg?

Bwyta yn Gymraeg?

Cael bath yn Gymraeg?

Golchi dillad yn Gymraeg?

Tacluso yn Gymraeg?

Chwarae Cuddio yn Gymraeg?

WORK OF THE SUMMER TERM

I.   The Names of Things
1. **Llestri** *(Dishes)*
2. **Symud** *(Movement)*
3. **Y Byd** *(The World)*
4. **Rhifolion** *(Numerals)*
5. **Lliwiau** *(Colours)*

II.   Sentence Patterns
1. Owning Things
   Mae _____ 'da fi. *(I have a _____.)*

2. Counting
   Sawl _____? *(How many _____?)*

3. Colours
   Pa liw yw hwn? *(What colour is this?)*

4. Who / What
   Pwy sy yna? *(Who is there?)*   **Pwy sy'n dod?** *(Who is coming?)*
   Beth sy yna? *(What is there?)*   **Beth sy'n dod?** *(What is coming?)*

5. Yes / No.
   Oes _____ yma? *(Is a _____ here?)*   **Oes.** *(Yes.)* / **Nac oes.** *(No.)*
   Oes _____ 'da ti? *(Do you have _____?)*   **Oes.** *(Yes.)* / **Nac oes.** *(No.)*

6. Describing Things
   Mae e'n dda (etc.) *(It's good [etc.])*

III.   The Books
8. **Beth mae Mabon yn ei wneud?**
9. **Mabon ar y mynydd**
10. **Mabon yn mynd i'r dre**

SUT
HOW

As you are preparing a meal hand the jam, toast, etc. to your child and ask her in Welsh to put it on the table.

In the case of the child who has only just learned how to walk, it would be wise to begin with something unbreakable or unspillable.

Brecwast *(Breakfast)*

Rho'r
Put the

tost	
jam	
creision ŷd *Corn Flakes*	

ar y ford, os gweli di'n dda. *please.*

Cinio/Te *(Dinner / Tea)*

Rho'r
Put the

sglodion *chips*	
finegr	
halen *salt*	

ar y ford, plîs.

PAM
WHY   *To teach your child:*
1. *The Welsh names of the food she eats every day.*
2. *The Welsh place words (prepositions)*

ar	**yn**	**wrth**	**dan**	**gyda**
on	*in*	*by*	*under*	*with*

3. *The pattern:* **Rho** _____. *(Put _____.)*
4. *How to lay the table.*

Some Further Practice

Further Hints p.118

	jam 	wrth **y tost.**	
Rho'r	llwy	yn **y basn siwgr.**	**'Na fe./Dyna fe.*** *That's it.*
	mat	dan **y marmalêd.**	*Note this* **Very Useful Phrase.**

Useful Information: *Things your child can put on the table (more or less safely)*

Brecwast *(Breakfast)*

creision ŷd		**jam**	
tost		**marmalêd**	
menyn		**mêl**	

Cinio/Te *(Dinner/Tea)*

bara		**pupur a halen**		**banana**	
bara menyn		**saws**		**ffrwythau**	
caws		**afal**		**bisgedi**	
sglodion/tsips 		**oren**		**creision**	
finegr					

Gyda *(With)—another handy place word (***Efo*** in North Wales)*

	pupur	**halen.**	
	afalau	**bananas.**	
Rho'r *Put the*	**caws**	**gyda'r** *with the* **menyn.**	**'Na fe./Dyna fe.** *That's it.*
	creision	**bisgedi.**	

71

22

LLESTRI: GOSOD Y FORD
Dishes: Laying the Table

SUT
HOW

When you lay the table hand the mats, pieces of cutlery, etc. to your child one at a time and show him in Welsh how to put them at each place.

In the case of the youngest children work with only one or two categories (mats and spoons perhaps) the first few times.

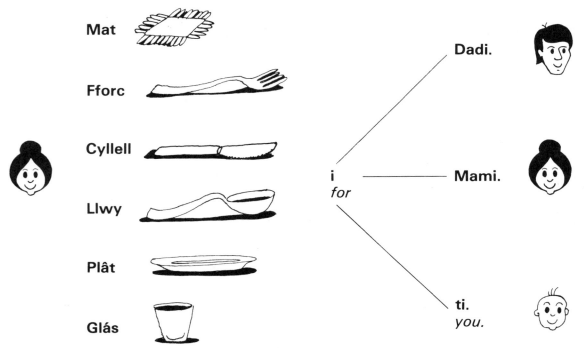

Mat		
Fforc		**Dadi.**
Cyllell		
Llwy	**i** *for*	**Mami.**
Plât		
Glás		**ti.** *you.*

PAM
WHY To teach your child:
1. *The Welsh names of the dishes, cutlery, etc. that he uses every day.*
2. *How to lay the table.*

Once your child begins to repeat the Welsh words after you, he should say:

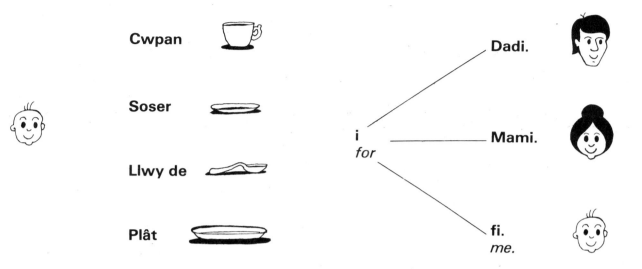

Cwpan

Soser

Llwy de

Plât

i
for

Dadi.

Mami.

fi.
me.

Llestri *(Dishes)*

jwg

basn siwgr

llwy

glás

tebot

plât

fforc

cyllell

cwpan

soser

llwy de

dysgl

A Table Laying Song

(Tune: "Polly put the kettle on")

> **Rhowch y lliain (etc.) ar y ford (3)**
> *Put the cloth (etc.) on the table*

> **I ni gael te.**
> *For us to have tea.*

Note:

-wch *is added to the verb stem when you are giving a command to*

> 1) More than one person.
> 2) One person if you don't know him very well.

23.
LLESTRI: GOLCHI'R LLESTRI
Dishes: Washing the Dishes

SUT
HOW

As you are washing the dishes allow your child to wash and dry anything that's unbreakable and safe.

Golcha'r badell ffrio nawr.

y badell ffrio

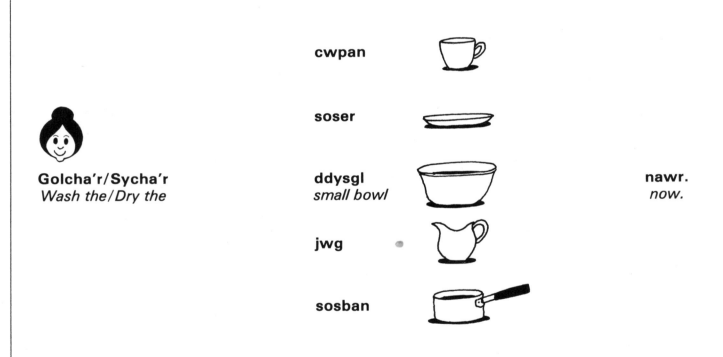

Golcha'r/Sycha'r
Wash the/Dry the

cwpan

soser

ddysgl
small bowl

jwg

sosban

nawr.
now.

PAM
WHY To give your child the fun of water play.

To teach your child:

1. The Welsh names of the dishes and cutlery that she uses every day.

2. The sentence pattern:
   Golcha _____. / *Wash* _____.   / **Sycha** _____. / *Dry* _____.

3. How to wash the dishes.

Cân Olchi'r Llestri   *A Dish-Washing Song*

Further Hints p.120

This is the perfect moment to introduce the last of the 3 most important Yes/No sentence patterns to your child **altogether painlessly.** *You simply sing (to the tune of "The farmer wants a wife"):*

Oes cwpan yn y sinc?
Is (there) a cup in the sink?

Oes cwpan yn y sinc?

Oes oes oes oes
Yes yes yes yes

Mae cwpan yn y sinc.
A cup is in the sink.

Oes dysgl yn y dŵr?
Is (there) a bowl in the water?

Oes dysgl yn y dŵr?

Nac oes, nac oes*
No   no

'Sdim** dysgl yn y dŵr.**
A bowl isn't in the water.

*Pronounced **Nag oes**
**'Sdim = Does dim

Y Gegin *(The Kitchen)*

A Further Suggestion

Naturally you can vary the above song to suit the occasion. If you want to turn it into a table laying song, for example, you can sing:

Oes cwpan ar y ford?
Is (there) a cup on the table?

Llyfr yr Wythnos

**Beth mae Mabon
yn ei wneud?**

ANOTHER BONUS (OR TWO)

1. Questions which parents like to ask

Beth yw dy enw di?
What is your name?

Ble 'wyt ti'n byw?
Where do you live?

2. A question which parents (and nursery school teachers) like to ask

Wyt ti'n hoffi _____?
Do you like _____?

SUT
HOW

Play this simple form of Follow-the-leader with your child. Say what you're doing as you perform the actions for him to copy, and encourage him to repeat the key word after you.

'Wy'n neidio !

'Wy'n
I am

sefyll. *standing.*		
cerdded. *walking.*		
rhedeg. *running.*		
troi. *turning.*		
neidio. *jumping.*		
gorwedd. *lying down.*		

sefyll

cerdded

rhedeg

troi

neidio

rhedeg

PAM

WHY   To teach your child:

Action words in Welsh and the actions that go with them.

Common Welsh describing words.

Here are some more action words to use in the game.

Further Hints p.121

'Wy'n
I'm

eistedd.
sitting.

codi.
getting up.

hercian.
hopping.

sgipio.
skipping.

'Wy'n
I'm

plygu.
bending.

cropian.
crawling.

martsio.
marching.

dawnsio.
dancing.

Good Advice for the Pregnant Mother

Action words can also be taught by relaxing comfortably on the sofa and looking at a book with your child. You simply say:

Beth mae e'n (ei) wneud?
What is he doing?

Nofio.
Swimming.

Hedfan.
Flying.

Beth mae hi'n (ei) wneud?
What is she doing?

Dringo.
Climbing.

Chwarae.
Playing.

Beth mae'n nhw'n (ei) wneud?
What are they doing?

Llefain./Crio.
Crying.

Chwerthin.
Laughing.

Note: *The **ei** is said so quickly that it's often scarcely heard.*

Here are two games which you might want to play occasionally in your group meetings.

1. Mr. Blaidd *(Mr. Wolf)*

The group leader or a mother (and child) is **Mr. Blaidd. Mr. Blaidd** *walks slowly towards the far end of the room while the mothers and children follow him, saying:*

Beth yw'r amser, Mr. Blaidd?
What is the time, Mr. Wolf?

Un o'r gloch.
One o'clock.

Beth yw'r amser, Mr. Blaidd?

Dau o'r gloch.
Two o'clock.

After reaching **tri o'r gloch** *or* **pedwar o'r gloch:**

Beth yw'r amser, Mr. Blaidd?

Amser cinio!
Dinner time!

Mothers and children run away and **Mr. Blaidd** *chases them. The one he catches (or anyone) is the next* **Mr. Blaidd.**

2. Mae'r Ffermwr Eisiau Gwraig *(The Farmer Wants a Wife)*

*One mother and child play the **ffermwr** and stand in the middle of the circle. The rest hold hands and move around them singing (to the same tune as that of the English version):*

Mae'r ffermwr eisiau gwraig.
The farmer wants a wife.
Mae'r ffermwr eisiau gwraig.
Hei ho di hei di ho
Mae'r ffermwr eisiau gwraig.

*The **ffermwr** chooses the **gwraig** (another mother and child). And so on.*

Mae'r wraig eisiau babi . . .
The wife wants a baby . . .

Mae'r babi eisiau nyrs . . .
The baby wants a nurse . . .

Mae'r nyrs eisiau ci . . .
The nurse wants a dog . . .

Mae'r ci eisiau asgwrn . . .
The dog wants a bone . . .

Mae pawb yn b'yta'r asgwrn . . .
Everyone eats the bone . . .

*Everyone runs towards the **asgwrn**, but the mother lifts her child safely up into the air.*

25
Y TYWYDD
The Weather

SUT
HOW

Comment on the weather to your child when she gets up in the morning and at any other appropriate moment during the day.

Mae'n braf.
It's fine.

Mae'n bwrw eira.
It's snowing.

Mae'n dwym.
It's warm.

Mae'n wyntog.
It's windy.

Mae'n ddiflas.
It's miserable.

Mae'n bwrw glaw.
It's raining.

Mae'n oer.
It's cold.

Mae'n gymylog.
It's cloudy.

PAM
WHY   To teach your child:
1.   To be aware of the weather and its consequences (wearing a jumper or Wellies or the like).
2.   How to talk about the weather in Welsh.

Yr Awyr (The Sky)

Further Hints p.122

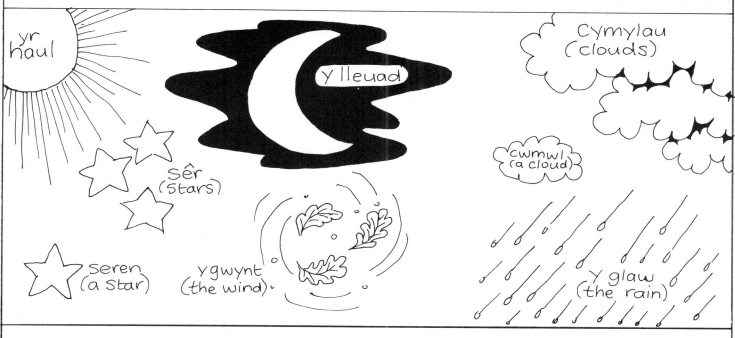

yr haul

y lleuad

Cymylau (clouds)

cwmwl (a cloud)

Sêr (stars)

seren (a star)

y gwynt (the wind)

y glaw (the rain)

Useful Information: *This is how you say "It's fine today." or "It's fine this morning."*

Mae'n braf heddi'. *It's fine today.*		**Mae'n braf y bore 'ma.** *It's fine this morning.*
Mae'n bwrw glaw heddi'.		**Mae'n bwrw glaw y bore 'ma.**
Mae'n oer heddi'.		**Mae'n oer y bore 'ma.**
Mae'n dwym heddi'.		**Mae'n dwym y bore 'ma.**
Mae'n dwym iawn heddi'. *It's very warm / hot today.*		**Mae'n dwym iawn y bore 'ma.**

Note	**Important!**
heddiw *(today)* is pronounced **heddi'** *(S. Wales)* **heddiw** *(N. Wales)*	*One of the first things babies learn to point to is the light. In Welsh you say:* **Ble mae'r golau?** *Where is the light?* **Fanna!** *There!*

SUT
HOW

Here is a game to be played when you go out shopping or on a walk around the neighbourhood.

On rainy days you might want to play it by simply standing in the window and looking outside.

 Beth sy ar yr heol?
What is on the road?

	car		
	ci		
Oes *Is there a*	**menyw** *woman*		**yma?/yno?** *here?/there?*
	lori		
	siop		

Oes./Nac oes.*
Yes./No.

*Pronounced
Nag oes.*

PAM
WHY   To teach your child:
1.   To observe the world around him.
2.   The Welsh names of everyday things in town.
3.   The sentence pattern:
   Oes _____?   **Oes./Nac oes.**
   Is a _____?   *Yes./No.*

This is also an excellent game to play when you are window shopping.

Beth sy yn y ffenest?
What is in the window?

Y Siop Deganau *(The Toy Shop)*

Oes
Is there a

trên	
tŷ dol	
pêl	
gêm	

yma?
here?

Oes./Nac oes.

Y Dre *(The Town)*

Beth sy yn y ffenest?

Llyfr yr Wythnos

Y Siop Ddillad *(The Clothes Shop)*

Oes

ffrog	
siwmper	
trowsus	
pais	

yma?

Oes./Nac oes.

**Mabon
ar y mynydd**

SUT
HOW

1. Play this game on drives or walks in the country.
2. Don't forget to say:

   Edrych ar _____!
   Look at _____!

   Wyt ti'n gweld _____?
   Do you see _____?

   from time to time too.

 Beth sy yn y cae?
What is in the field?

	ceffyl 	
Oes *Is / Are*	**tractor**	**yno?** *there?*
	defaid	

Oes./Nac oes.*
Yes. / No.

Beth sy yn y goeden?
What is in the tree?

	wiwer 	
Oes *Is*	**'deryn**	**yno?** *there?*
	nyth *nest*	

*Pronounced **Nag** oes.

PAM
WHY To teach your child:
1. To observe the world around her.
2. The Welsh names of everyday things in the country.
3. The sentence pattern:

   Oes _____?   **Oes./Nac oes.**
   Is a _____?   *Yes. / No.*

The game can be played equally well when you are looking at pictures in books and magazines.

 Beth sy yn y llun?
What is in the picture?

 Oes

castell

adar

afon

bryn

yma?

 Oes./Nac oes.

Y Wlad *(The Country)*

Remember to say also from time to time:

 Beth yw hwn?

 Pili-pala!

 Coeden!

 Cwningen!

 Ble mae'r

bont?

llong?

fuwch?

Fan hyn!
Here!

Fanna!
There!

28
PERCHEN PETHAU
Owning Things

SUT
HOW

As you look at a catalogue or magazine with your child, point out and name the things you both own.

*ysgol = ladder or school

 Beth sy 'da ti?
What do you have?

	tedi		
	tŷ dol		
Mae *You have*	**pêl**		**'da ti.***
	llong *a ship*		
	llestri te *teaset*		

North Wales — **gen ti.*

PAM
WHY To teach your child:
1. The Welsh names of his toys and common objects about the house.
2. The sentence pattern:

   Mae _____ 'da fi / ti / ni.
   I / you / we have _____.
   (Literally: _____ *is with me / you / us.*)

Mae
I've got

lori

jig-so

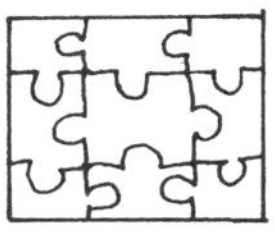

trên

beic

ceffyl

'da fi.*

*North Wales — **gen i.**

Oes.
Yes.

A Useful Tip

If you can't remember the Welsh word for the object in question, you can say:

Mae hwn 'da ti.
You've got this.

Mae hwnna 'da ti.
You have that.

Mae un fel 'na 'da ti.
You have one like that.

Llyfr yr Wythnos

Mabon yn mynd i'r dre

Gêm

Your child hides something behind his back and you try to guess what it is.

car

bloc

Oes
Do you have

cwpan

'da ti?

hosan

llyfr

Nac oes.*

Nac oes.

Nac oes.

Nac oes.

Oes!
Pronounced
Nag *oes.*

A FINAL BONUS

Some Exceptionally Useful Phrases

Pwy sy
Who is

yna?
there?

'n dod?
coming?

'n barod?
ready?

Fi!
Me!

Beth sy

yma?

ar y ford?

'n goch?
red?

'da ti?

Pêl!

An Afterthought

Neb *(No one)*		**Dim byd** *(Nothing)*	
 Pwy sy yna?	Neb!	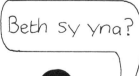 Beth sy yna?	Dim byd!

Useful Information:	*Here are more questions that you might want to ask when you are reading a story.*	 **Hugan Goch Fach** *Little Red Riding Hood*	**Mr. Blaidd** *Mr. Wolf*

Pwy sy yna?
Who is there?

 Hugan Goch Fach.

Beth sy 'da hi?
What does she have?

 Basged.
A basket.

Beth sy yn y fasged?
What is in the basket?

 Teisen a llaeth.
A cake and milk.

Pwy sy'n dod?
Who is coming?

 Mr. Blaidd!

Beth sy yma?
What is here?

 Tŷ Mam-gu.
Grandmother's house.

Pwy sy yn y gwely?
Who is in the bed?

 Mam-gu.

(To be continued)

1. Count steps, buttons, anything that comes naturally with your child.
2. Sing counting songs, such as "Un bys, dau fys" (see p.4) together.

1 Un

2 Dau

3 Tri

4 Pedwar

5 Pump

6 Chwech

7 Saith

8 Wyth

9 Naw

10 Deg

PAM
WHY To teach your child:
        To count in Welsh.

Children under three like to count by linking numbers together into a kind of chant. Only very gradually do they come to understand what numbers mean and how they are used. Here are some ways you can use to show them:

Losin *(Sweets)*

Un i ti **ac un i fi.**
One for you   and one for me.

Un dau i ti **ac un dau i fi.**

Tost *(Toast)*

Dyma

 un i ti ac

un, dau i fi ac

un, dau, tri i Dadi.

Ceir *(Cars)*

Sawl car sy 'da ti?
How many cars do you have?

Un, dau, tri, pedwar!

Sglodion *(Chips)*

Sawl un sy ar ôl?
How many are left?

**Un, dau, tri, pedwar,
pump, chwech, saith!**

For Parents Only: *Note how numbers above 10 are formed.*

11
un deg un

12
un deg dau

13
un deg tri

24
dau ddeg pedwar

35
tri deg pump

46
pedwar deg chwech

57
pum deg saith

68
chwe deg wyth

100
cant

30
Y LLIWIAU/DISGRIFIO PETHAU
The Colours/Describing Things

SUT
HOW

You can teach colours and other describing words to your child while painting or colouring, looking at books, playing with blocks and other toys, sorting the laundry, or in almost any circumstances.

*But in the case of colours remember that children are often physically unable to distinguish between them before the age of 4, and be prepared to ask **and** answer your questions in the early years.*

 Pa liw yw hwn?
What colour is this?

Coch*	**Oren**	**Du**
Melyn	**Gwyrdd**	**Gwyn**
Glas	**Piws/Porffor**	**Brown**
		Llwyd

*Please colour in the squares (see p. 95)

PAM
WHY *To teach your child:*
  1. The Welsh names of colours.
  2. Other common Welsh describing words.

You might also want to ask:

Pa liw yw'r
What colour is the

 ci?

Gwyn.

gath?

Du.

ceffyl?

Du a gwyn.
Black and white.

Useful Information

pinc/yn binc	*pink*	**piws/yn biws**	*purple*
coch/yn goch	*red*	**porffor/yn borffor**	*purple*
oren/yn oren	*orange*	**brown/yn frown**	*brown*
melyn/yn felyn	*yellow*	**du/yn ddu**	*black*
gwyrdd/yn wyrdd	*green*	**gwyn/yn wyn**	*white*
glas/yn las	*blue*	**llwyd/yn llwyd**	*grey*

Remember: *In Welsh describing sentences the word* **yn/'n** *is necessary but can't be translated.*

Ci gwyn.
A white dog.

Mae'r ci'n wyn.
The dog is white.

Mae e'n wyn.
He's white.

Cath ddu.
A black cat.

Mae'r gath yn ddu.
The cat is black.

Mae hi'n ddu.
She's black.

More Useful Information

The poem "Y Lliwiau" in **Mi Welais Jac-y-Do** *(no. 12) will help you to teach your child the Welsh names for colours and for other things as well.*

Further Hints

1
Y CANEUON
The Songs

Useful Information *for your group sessions.*

Preliminaries	Conclusion

Things your leader may say before you sing.

Ydych chi'n barod?
Are you ready?

Barod?
Ready?

Un—dau—tri . . .
One—two—three . .

Things your leader may say when you finish the song.

Da iawn!
Very good!

Hyfryd!
Lovely!

Ardderchog!
Excellent!

More Preliminaries

Songs 3 and 4 can be used to teach the describing words:

ara'	**cyflym**	**tawel**	**swnllyd**	**uchel**	**isel**
slow	*quick*	*quiet*	*noisy*	*high*	*low*

3. *The children love to imitate the group leader and their mothers, twirling their hands slowly and then quickly, etc., as the leader gives directions.*

Trowch eich dwylo'n ara', ara', ara'/yn gyflym, gyflym, gyflym, gyflym!
Turn your hands slowly, slowly, slowly / quickly, quickly, quickly, quickly!

Curwch eich dwylo'n dawel, dawel, dawel—shh!/yn swnllyd, swnllyd, swnllyd!
Clap your hands quietly, quietly, quietly / noisily, noisily, noisily!

Chwifiwch eich dwylo lan yn yr awyr yn uchel/i lawr ar y llawr yn isel.
Wave your hands up in the air, high / down on the ground, low.

4. *The second time through the song sing slowly at the beginning and then faster and faster.*

Y tro yma *yn ara'* **ar y dechrau ac wedyn** *yn gyflym.*
This time **slowly** *at the beginning and then* **fast**.

Yn ara' **ac wedyn** *yn gyflym.*
Slowly *and then* **fast**.

2
TRWY'R DYDD
Through the Day

Bore

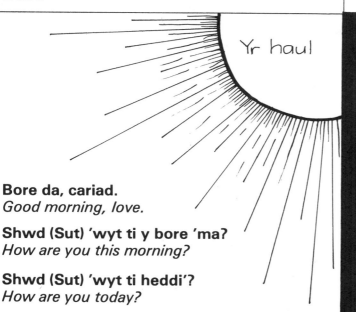

Yr haul

Bore da, cariad.
Good morning, love.

Shwd (Sut) 'wyt ti y bore 'ma?
How are you this morning?

Shwd (Sut) 'wyt ti heddi'?
How are you today?

Nos

Y lleuad

seren

Rho gusan i Mami/Dadi.
Give a kiss to Mammy/Daddy.

Rho gusan i fi.
Give me a kiss.

Nos da, cariad.
Good night, love.

Useful Information

You will have noticed by now that

In English we say	In Welsh (Yn Gymraeg)
good *morning*	*bore* **da**
good *night*	*nos* **da**
breakfast *time*	*amser* **brecwast**
tea*time*	*amser* **te**

That is, in Welsh the describing word comes **after** the thing described.

Adults have to learn this rule consciously. Your child will come to know it unconsciously as you repeat these phrases to her every day.

Geirfa *(Vocabulary)*

bore (m)—*morning*
nos (f)—*night*
cariad (m)—*love*
amser (m)—*time*
brecwast (m)—*breakfast*
cinio (m)—*dinner*
te (m)—*tea*
swper (m)—*supper*
gwely (m)—*bed*
cusan (m)—*kiss*

da—*good*

i/fi/mi—*I, me*
ti—*you (one person, 'familiar' —use when you are talking to children, members of the family, close friends)*

rwyt ti—*you are*

rhoi—*to give, put*
  rho—*give, put (command— 1 person, 'familiar')*
codi—*to get up, raise*

cysgu—*to sleep*

i—*to, for*

heddiw—*today (pronounced* **heddi'** *in S. Wales)*
y (bore) yma—*this (morning)*

Sut?—*How? (pronounced* **Shwd?** *in S. Wales)*

3
CWRTEISI (etc.)
Courtesy

Useful Information

For those of you who are currently involved in toilet training

1. The basic question:

Wyt ti eisiau* mynd i'r tŷ bach?
Do you want to go to the toilet?

*Pronounced **ee-sheh** *in S. Wales;* **ee-sho** *in N. Wales.*

Na!

2. Or—if there is need for haste:

Mynd i'r tŷ bach?

Tŷ bach?

Yn gyflym, gyflym!
Quickly!

4
Y CORFF 1
The Body 1

More Useful Information: *To ask your child "Where is **your** head?" etc. you say:*

1. The Head	2. The Rest of the Body

1. The Head

Ble mae dy
Where is your

ben?

lygad?

drwyn?

glust?

geg?

2. The Rest of the Body

fraich?

law?

fys?

Ble mae dy
Where is your

gefn?

ben ôl?

goes?

droed?

A Word of Explanation

Dy *(Your)*	Eich *(Your)*

Dy *(Your)*

*To be used when you speak to **one** person if that person is a **child**, a **member of the family**, or **close friend**.*

Eich *(Your)*

To be used when you speak to:
1. **More** *than one person.*
2. **One** *person if you don't know him very well.*

Geirfa

corff (m)—*body*

pen (m)—*head*
llygad (f)—*eye*
  llygaid—*eyes*
clust, y glust (f)—*ear*
  clustiau—*ears*
trwyn (m)—*nose*
ceg, y geg (f)—*mouth*

braich, y fraich (f)—*arm*
  breichiau—*arms*
llaw (f)—*hand*
  dwylo—*hands*
bys (m)—*finger*
  bysedd—*fingers*

bola (m)—*stomach*

cefn (m)—*back*
pen ôl (m)—*bottom*

coes, y goes (f)—*leg*
  coesau—*legs*
troed, y droed (f)—*foot*
  traed—*feet*

5
ANIFEILIAID Y FFERM
Animals of the Farm

Useful Information: *You might also want to ask:*

fuwch

ci

gath

ceffyl

Beth mae'r
What does the

ddafad

yn (ei) ddweud?
say?

mochyn

afr

hwyaden

iâr

ceiliog

Mw Mw!

W-wff W-wff!

Miaw!

Neee!

Me Me!

Rhoch Rhoch!

Me Me!

Cwac Cwac!

Clwc Clwc!

Cocadwdldww!

Note:

Beth mae'r fuwch yn *ei* ddweud?   *What is **it** the cow is saying? (literally)*

*The **ei** is said so quickly that it is often scarcely heard in spoken Welsh:*

Beth mae'r fuwch yn ddweud?   **Beth mae'r ceffyl yn ddweud?**
What is the cow saying?   *What does the horse say?*

Geirfa

ci (m)—*dog*
  cŵn—*dogs*
cath, y gath (f)—*cat*
  cathod—*cats*
ceffyl (m)—*horse*
  ceffylau—*horses*
dafad, y ddafad (f)—*sheep*
  defaid—*sheep*
      (more than one)

buwch, y fuwch (f)—*cow*
  da—*cattle (S. Wales)*
  gwartheg—*cattle*
    (N. Wales)
mochyn (m)—*pig*
  moch—*pigs*
gafr, yr afr (f)—*goat*
  geifr—*goats*
ceiliog (m)—*cockerel*

iâr (f)—*hen*
  ieir—*hens*
cyw (bach) (m)—*(little) chick*
  cywion—*chicks*
hwyaden (f)—*duck*
  hwyaid—*ducks*
gŵydd, yr ŵydd (f)—*goose*
  gwyddau—*geese*

6
GOLCHI DWYLO
Washing Hands

Variations/Additions

Dere 'ma i olchi dwylo.
Come here to wash (your) hands.

'Wyt ti'n frwnt.
You are dirty.

'Wyt ti'n wlyb.
You are wet.

Dere 'ma i sychu dwylo.
Come here to dry (your) hands.

'Wyt ti'n lân nawr.
You are clean now.

'Wyt ti'n sych nawr.
You are dry now.

Cân Olchi Dwylo

*The song can be varied as follows,
according to circumstances.*

Dyma'r ffordd i olchi wyneb . . .
Here's the way to wash (your) face . . .

Dyma'r ffordd i frwsio dannedd . . .
Here's the way to brush (your) teeth . . .

Yn hwyr yn y nos.
Late in the night.

Geirfa

dŵr (m)—*water*	**brwnt**—*dirty*	**brwsio**—*to brush*
lliain (m)—*towel*	**glân**—*clean*	**golchi**—*to wash*
sebon (m)—*soap*	**gwlyb**—*wet*	**sychu**—*to dry*
	sych—*dry*	

7
DILLAD
Clothes

Variations/Additions

Gwisga dy
Put on your

 het.

 got.

 sgarff.

Tynna dy
Take off your

 gap.

 fenig.

 welis.

Useful Information

Often young children are eager to help tend the baby by fetching his / her clothes for you. This is the way you ask for help in Welsh.

Cer i ôl
Go to fetch

clwt
nappy

fest

dillad nos
pyjamas

y babi, plîs.
of the baby, please.

Geirfa

dillad—*clothes*

pants (m)—*underpants*
fest (f)—*vest*
pais, y bais (f)—*petticoat*

ffrog (f)—*dress*
sgert (f)—*skirt*
blows, y flows (f)—*blouse*
ffedog (f)—*apron*
cardigan, y gardigan (f)—
   cardigan

crys (m)—*shirt*
trowsus (m)—*trousers*
   trowsus byr (m)—*shorts*
tei (m)—*tie*

siwmper (f)—*jumper*
siaced (f)—*jacket*

teits (m)—*tights*
hosan (f)—*sock, stocking*
   'sanau—*socks, stockings*
   (pronounced **saneh**)
esgid (f)—*shoe*
   'sgidiau—*shoes*
   (pronounced **sgidieh**)

dillad nos—*pyjamas*
gwisg nos, y wisg nos (f)—
   nightgown
sliper (f)—*slipper*
   sliperi—*slippers*

clwt (m)—*nappy*
   clytiau—*nappies*
neisied (f)—*handkerchief*
   neisiedon—*handkerchiefs*
cot, y got (f)—*coat*
cot law, y got law (f)—
   raincoat
het (f)—*hat*
cap (m)—*cap*
maneg, y faneg (f)—*glove*
   menig—*gloves*
sgarff (f)—*scarf*
ymbarél (m)—*umbrella*

gwisgo—*to put on, wear*
tynnu—*to take off, pull*

Note: *Notice that the clothes most obviously belonging to a boy are masculine and that practically everything else is feminine.*

8
BWYD: AMSER BRECWAST
Food: Breakfast Time

Useful Information *for those mornings when you're in a hurry*

B'yta dy
Eat your

uwd

greision ŷd

dost

gig moch

wy

plîs.

Yfa dy
Drink your

sudd oren

laeth

de

goffi

ddŵr
water

nawr.
now.

Geirfa

bwyd (m)—*food*
brecwast (m)—*breakfast*

sudd oren (m)—*orange juice*
uwd (m)—*porridge*
creision ŷd—*cornflakes*
sirial (m)—*cereal*

tost (m)—*toast*
menyn (m)—*butter*

marmalêd (m)—*marmalade*
jam (m)—*jam*
mêl (m)—*honey*

cig moch (m)—*bacon*
bara saim (m)—*fried bread*
wy (m)—*egg*
wy wedi (ei) ferwi—*boiled egg*
wy wedi (ei) ffrio—*fried egg*
wy wedi (ei) falu—*scrambled egg*

wy wedi (ei) botsio—*poached egg*

llaeth (m)—*milk*
te (m)—*tea*
coffi (m)—*coffee*
siwgr (m)—*sugar*

bwyta—*to eat (pronounced b'yta in S. Wales)*
yfed—*to drink*

9
BWYD: AMSER CINIO
Food: Dinner Time

Useful Phrases

'Na ddigon.
That's enough.

Mae'n dwym.
It's hot.

Wedi mynd.
All gone.

Whether you dish out food to the family in the kitchen or at the table, make a habit of saying:

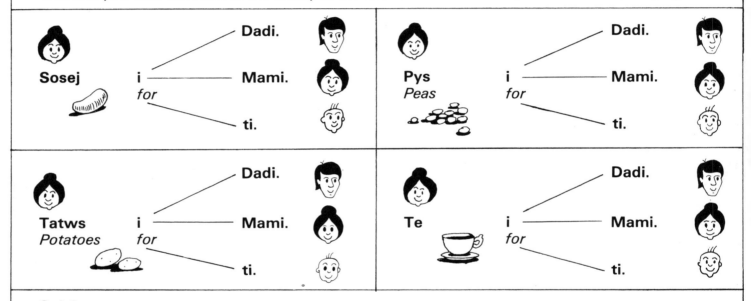

Sosej — i — Dadi. / Mami. / ti.
for

Pys — i — Dadi. / Mami. / ti.
Peas *for*

Tatws — i — Dadi. / Mami. / ti.
Potatoes *for*

Te — i — Dadi. / Mami. / ti.
for

Geirfa

cinio (m)—*dinner*

cawl (m)—*soup*
wy (m)—*egg*
  wyau—*eggs*
sosej (f)—*sausage*
selsig (f)—*sausage*
pastai, y bastai (f)—*pie, pasty*
pysgodyn (m)—*fish (one)*
  pysgod—*fish(es)*

pys—*peas*
ffa coch—*baked beans*
sbageti—*spaghetti*
tatws—*potatoes*
  taten, y daten (f)—*potato*

sglodion/sglods/tsips—*chips*

bara (m)—*bread*
torth, y dorth (f)—*loaf*
  torth wen—*white loaf*
  torth frown—*brown loaf*
bara menyn (m)—*bread and butter*
brechdan, y frechdan (f)— *sandwich*
  brechdanau—*sandwiches*
caws (m)—*cheese*

finegr (m)—*vinegar*
saws (m)—*sauce*
pupur (m)—*pepper*
halen (m)—*salt*

afal (m)—*apple*
  afalau—*apples*
banana (m)—*banana*
  bananas—*bananas*
oren (m)—*orange*
  orennau—*oranges*

creision—*crisps*
bisgïen, y fisgïen (f)—*biscuit*
  bisgedi—*biscuits*
losin—*sweets*
siocled (m)—*chocolate*

diod, y ddiod (f)—*drink*
dŵr (m)—*water*
pop (m)—*pop*

10
BWYD: AMSER TE
Food: Teatime

Variations/Additions

These questions require your child to name the thing she wants in Welsh.
Begin with Step 1 (showing your child the things you are offering her the first few times). When you think that she has learned the Welsh words for whatever she is likely to want, move on to Step 2.

Step 1	Step 2

Step 1

Wyt ti eisiau
Do you want

Weetabix
Weetabix

afal
apple

creision
crisps

llaeth
milk

neu uwd?
or porridge?

neu oren?
or

neu losin?
or sweets?

neu de?
or tea?

Step 2

Beth 'wyt ti (ei) eisiau
What do you want

i frecwast?
for breakfast?

i ginio?
for dinner?

i de?
for tea?

NOTE: *eisiau is the only Welsh verb (doing word) that does **not** require* **yn/'n** *before it in present time.*

Wyt ti'n mynd?
Are you going?

Wyt ti'n gweld?
Do you see?

Wyt ti eisiau _____?
Do you want _____?

Useful Questions

Wyt ti eisiau

bisgïen arall?
another biscuit?

afal arall?
another apple?

Wyt ti eisiau

rhagor o jam?
more jam?

rhagor o laeth?
more milk?

Geirfa

te (m)—*tea*
swper (m)—*supper*

cig (m)—*meat*
cig eidion (m)—*beef*
cig oen (m)—*lamb*
cig llo (m)—*veal*
porc (m)—*pork*
ham (m)—*ham*
stêc (m)—*steak*
ffowlyn (m)—*chicken*
grefi (m)—*gravy*

llysiau—*vegetables*
moron—*carrots*
bresych—*cabbage*

blodfresych—*cauliflower*
winwns—*onions*
madarch—*mushrooms*
maip—*swedes*
pannas—*parsnips*
letys—*lettuce*
tomato (m)—*tomato*
cucumer (m)—*cucumber*
salad (m)—*salad*
reis (m)—*rice*

ffrwythau—*fruit*
peren, y beren (f)—*pear*
  pêr—*pears*
grawnwin—*grapes*
mefus—*strawberries*

eirinen (f)—*plum*
  eirin—*plums*
cnau—*nuts*

pwdin (m)—*pudding*
pwdin reis (m)—*rice pudding*
hufen iâ (m)—*ice cream*
tarten, y darten (f)—*tart*
  tarten afalau—*apple tart*
  tarten riwbob—*rhubarb tart*
  tarten fwyar duon—*blackberry tart*
cwstard (m)—*custard*
teisen, y deisen (f)—*cake*
  teisennau—*cakes*

11
Y CORFF 2
The Body 2

More Useful Information: *Here is the way that you ask "Where is your hair?" etc.*

1. From head to shoulders:

Ble mae dy
Where is your

wallt?

wyneb?

ddannedd?

dafod?

wefus?

foch?

wddwg?

 Fan hyn!

2. From the shoulders down:

Ble mae dy
Where is your

ysgwydd?

frest?

benelin?

fawd?

ewin?

ben-lin?

 Fan hyn!

 Ble mae   **bysedd dy draed?** **Fan hyn!**

Geirfa

gwallt (m)—*hair*
wyneb (m)—*face*
boch, y foch (f)—*cheek*
  bochau—*cheeks*
gwefus, y wefus (f)—*lip*
  gwefusau—*lips*
dant (m)—*tooth*
  dannedd—*teeth*
tafod (m)—*tongue*

gwddwg (m)—*neck, throat*
ysgwydd (f)—*shoulder*
  ysgwyddau—*shoulders*
brest, y frest (f)—*chest*

penelin (m)—*elbow*
bawd (m)—*thumb*
ewin (m)—*fingernail*
  ewinedd—*fingernails*

pen-lin, y ben-lin (f)—*knee*
  penliniau—*knees*
bys troed (m)—*toe*
  bysedd troed—*toes*
bys dy droed—*your toe*
  bysedd dy draed—*your toes*

12
CAEL BATH
Having a Bath

Useful Information

If your child needs your help with washing in the bath, you may want to say:

'Wy'n golchi*
I'm washing

dy wyneb.

dy fraich.

dy gefn.

dy droed.

Obviously you can substitute **sychu (to dry)
at the appropriate moment.*

When your child begins to wash himself you can say:

'Wyt ti'n golchi
You're washing

dy glust.

dy frest.

dy fola.

dy ben-lin.

Useful Phrases in the Bath

I mewn â ti!
In with you!

Ma's â ti!
Out with you!

Cau dy lygaid.
Close your eyes.

Paid â sblasio!
Don't splash!

13
LLYFRAU
Books

Useful Information

If you want to ask a question about more than one thing, you say:

Adar.
Birds.

Beth yw'r rhain?
What are these?

'Sanau.
Socks.

Blodau.
Flowers.

Tatws.
Potatoes.

Pysgod.
Fish.

Beth yw'r rheina?
What are those?

'Sgidiau.
Shoes.

Coed.
Trees.

Bisgedi.
Biscuits.

Geirfa

llyfr (m)—*book*
  llyfrau—*books*
cân, y gân (f)—*song*
  caneuon—*songs*

hwn/hon—*this (masculine / feminine)*
hwnna/honna—*that (masculine / feminine)*

y rhain—*these*
y rheina—*those*

darllen—*to read*
canu—*to sing*

mae—*is / are (after **Ble**, etc.)*
yw—*is / are (after **Pwy, Beth**, etc.)*

Ble?—*Where?*
Pwy?—*Who?*
Beth?—*What?*

a—*and (**ac** before vowels)*

DILLAD: GOLCHI
Clothes: Washing

Useful Information: *Here are 2 ways to use Welsh as you hang out the wash.*

1. Ask your child to hand the clothes to you.	2. Ask your child to hand the pegs to you.

siwmper Mami

Rho *Give*   **grys Dadi**   **i fi.** *to me.*

dy ffedog di

beg *a peg*

Rho *Give*   **un peg** *one peg*   **i Mami, plîs.** *to Mammy, please.*

ddau beg *two pegs*

Rho drowsus Dadi i fi.

y lein

Geirfa

siten (m)—*sheet*
  sitenni—*sheets*
blanced, y flanced (f)—*blanket*
  blancedi—*blankets*
cas gobennydd (m)—*pillowcase*
  casau gobennydd—*pillowcases*

lliain (bord) (m)—*tablecloth*
napcyn (m)—*serviette*
  napcynau—*serviettes*

gwlanen, y wlanen (f)—*flannel*
clwtyn (m)—*facecloth*
  clytiau—*facecloths*
lliain (m)—*towel*

llieiniau—*towels*

basged, y fasged (f)—*basket*
lein (ddillad) (f)—*clothesline*
peiriant golchi (m)—*washing machine*
sychydd (m)—*dryer*
peg (m)—*peg*
  pegiau—*pegs*

A Variation on the Game

See whether your child can go to a particular place in her bedroom by the time that you count to five.

y gwely

y ddesg

Cer at
Go to

y wal    os gweli di'n dda.

y ffenest

y silffoedd llyfrau
(*pronounced* **shilffoedd**)

Un — dau — tri — pedwar — pump!
1   2   3   4   5

Geirfa

gwely (m)—*bed*
cadair, y gadair (f)—*chair*
bord, y ford (f)—*table*
cwpwrdd (m)—*cupboard*
desg, y ddesg (f)—*desk*
biwrô (m)—*bureau*
drôr (m)—*drawer*

llun (m)—*picture*
  lluniau—*pictures*
silff (f)—*shelf* (pronounced
  shilff *in S. Wales*)
silff lyfrau (f)—*bookshelf*
silffoedd llyfrau—*bookcase*
gobennydd (m)—*pillow*

drws (m)—*door*
ffenest (f)—*window*
llawr (m)—*floor*
carped (m)—*carpet*
wal (f)—*wall*
  waliau—*walls*
nenfwd (f)—*ceiling*
cornel (m)—*corner*
golau (m)—*light*

DILLAD: TYNNU DILLAD
Clothes: Undressing

Useful Information

From about 12 months on some children like to help to undress themselves and can actually do it if the parent unfastens and partly pulls off the shoes, socks, etc. ahead of time. Here is the way that you can encourage your child to undress himself in Welsh.

het.

sgarff.

Tynna dy
Take off your   got.

'sgidiau.

'sanau.

Bachgen	Merch
Tynna dy drowsus. grys.	**Tynna dy** sgert. gardigan.

 DA IAWN!

17
TEGANAU: TACLUSO
Toys: Tidying Up

Useful Information

If you simply want to tell your child to put her toys "away" without specifying where, this is how you do it.

Rho'r
Put the

trên

llestri te

awyren

ceir

heibio, os gweli di'n dda.
away.

More Useful Information: *There are two possible approaches to tidying up with your child.*

1. The Diplomatic Approach

*Come to help Mammy, love.

2. The Undiplomatic Approach

*Put everything away! At once!

Geirfa

tegan (m)—*toy*
  teganau—*toys*

tedi (m)—*teddy*
dol/doli, y ddol/ddoli (f)—*doll*

pêl, y bêl (f)—*ball*
  peli—*balls*
llyfr (m)—*book*
  (pronounced **llyfyr**)
  llyfrau—*books*
bloc (m)—*block*
  blociau—*blocks*

gêm (f)—*game*
  gêmau—*games*
jig-so (m)—*jigsaw puzzle*

beic (m)—*bicycle*
ceffyl pren (m)—*rocking*
  (literally: *wooden*) *horse*
whilber (f)—*wheelbarrow*

tŷ dol (m)—*doll's house*
llestri te—*teaset (literally: tea dishes)*

car (m)—*car*
  ceir—*cars*
lori (f)—*lorry*
  loriau—*lorries*
trên (m)—*train*
ambiwlans (m)—*ambulance*
awyren (f)—*airplane*
  awyrennau—*airplanes*
llong (f)—*ship*
  llongau—*ships*

114

18
TEGANAU: CHWARAE
Toys: Playing

Useful Information

Mae'r bachgen yn y tŷ.
The boy is in the house.

Mae *e* **yn y tŷ.**
He *is in the house.*

Mae'r ferch yn y tŷ.
The girl is in the house.

Mae *hi* **yn y tŷ.**
She *is in the house.*

Mae'r llyfr dan y ford.
The book is under the table.

Mae *e* **dan y ford.**
It *is under the table.*

Mae'r bêl dan y ford.
The ball is under the table.

Mae *hi* **dan y ford.**
It *is under the table.*

Note:

Every person **or** *thing in Welsh is either masculine or feminine. Knowledge of which things are which will come to you and your child gradually with practice and over a period of time.*

Don't worry about making mistakes!

It is far better to refer to everything as **e** *(he) at the beginning than not to use the language at all.*

Geirfa

tŷ (m)—*house*
'stafell (f)—*room*
  'stafelloedd (f)—*rooms*

parlwr (m)—*parlour*
'stafell fyw (f)—*living room*
lolfa (f)—*lounge*

cegin, y gegin (f)—*kitchen*
'stafell fwyta (f)—*dining room*

'stafell wely (f)—*bedroom*
'stafell 'molchi (f)—*bathroom*
tŷ bach (m)—*lavatory*

pasej (m)—*passage*
grisiau—*stairs (N. Wales)*
  stâr—*stairs (S. Wales)*
cwts dan stâr (m)—*cupboard under the stairs*

lan llofft—*upstairs*
lawr llawr—*downstairs*

gardd, yr ardd (f)—*garden*

mynd—*to go*
  cer/cere—*go (command form—1 person, familiar)*
ôl/nôl—*to fetch*

mae—*is*
  mae e—*he is*
  mae hi—*she is*

dy ('stafell)/dy ('stafell) di—*your (room)*

19
GÊM: CUDDIO 1
Game: Hide and Seek 1

Useful Phrases (*when preparing to play* **Cuddio***)*

Cuddio 1	Cuddio 2 (*see p. 64*)

Cer i guddio.
Go to hide.

'Wy'n cau fy llygaid.
I'm closing my eyes.

Barod?
Ready?

Mae Tedi'n mynd i guddio.
Teddy is going to hide.

Cau dy lygaid.
Close your eyes.

Barod!
Ready!

Useful Information

By now we have encountered 2 of the 3 most important **Yes and No Questions** *that occur between parent and child.*

1.

Wyt ti eisiau llaeth?

Wyt ti dan y ford?

Wyt ti'n dod?
Are you coming?

 Ydw./Nac ydw.
Yes. / No.

2.

Nia

Ydy hi dan y ford?
Is she

'r ferch
the girl

Dewi'n

Ydy e'n dod?
Is he

'r bachgen yn
the boy

Ydy./Nac ydy.
Yes. / No.

Geirfa

celfi—*furniture*

soffa (f)—*sofa*
clustog, y glustog (f)—*pillow, cushion*
  clustogau—*pillows, cushions*
cadair, y gadair (f)—*chair*
  cadeiriau—*chairs*
bord, y ford (f)—*table*
  bordydd—*tables*

llen (f)—*curtain*
  llenni—*curtains*
carped (m)—*carpet*

tân (m)—*fire*
lle tân (m)—*fireplace*
silff ben tân (f)—*mantlepiece*

llun (m)—*picture*
  lluniau—*pictures*
piano (m)—*piano*
silff lyfrau (f)—*bookshelf*
silffoedd llyfrau—*bookcase*

telyn, y delyn (f)—*harp*
teledu (m)—*television set*

cloc (m)—*clock*
lamp (f)—*lamp*
golau (m)—*light*
  goleuadau—*lights*

ffenest (f)—*window*
  ffenestri—*windows*
drws (m)—*door*

Useful Information

mynd—*go, to go*	yn mynd—*go, going*
*rwy i'n/rydw i'n mynd—*I am going, go*	rydyn ni'n mynd—*we are going, go*
*rwyt ti'n mynd—*you are going, go*	rydych chi'n mynd—*you are going, go*
mae e'n/hi'n mynd—*he/she is going, goes*	maen nhw'n mynd—*they are going, go*
mae'r plentyn yn mynd—*the child is going, goes*	mae'r plant yn mynd—*the children are going, go*

*These are **written** forms. What you will hear people saying is:*

South Wales	**'wy'n mynd**	*North Wales*	**'dwi'n mynd**
	'yt ti'n mynd		**'wyt ti'n mynd**

Useful Information For The Garden (and elsewhere)

	Wedi cwympo? *([You've] fallen?)*	**Lan â ti!** *(Up with you!)*
		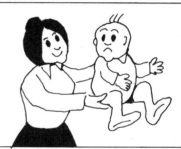
'Sdim ots. *(It doesn't matter.)*	**Paid â llefain.** *(Don't cry).*	**Popeth yn iawn.** *(Everything's okay.)*
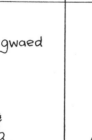		

Geirfa

gardd, yr ardd (f)—*garden*
  gerddi—*gardens*

blodyn (m)—*flower*
  blodau—*flowers*
llysiau—*vegetables*
gwair (m)—*grass*
coeden, y goeden (f)—*tree*
  coed—*trees*

deilen, y ddeilen (f)—*leaf*
  dail—*leaves*
llwyn (m)—*bush*
  llwyni—*bushes*

cwt (m)—*shed*
llwybr (m)—*path*
siglen (f)—*swing*
llithren (f)—*slide*
si-so (m)—*seesaw*

wal (f)—*wall*
perth, y berth (f)—*hedge*
  perthi—*hedges*

(a)deryn (m)—*bird*
  adar—*birds*
nyth (f)—*nest*
malwoden, y falwoden (f)—*snail*
  malwod—*snails*
mwydyn (m)—*worm*

Useful Information:

Your child probably enjoys helping you to put things away after shopping. This is how you do it in Welsh:

Dere i helpu Mami, cariad.
Come to help Mammy, love.

 **bag siopa**  **torth**  **tuniau**   **menyn**  **bisgedi**

Rho'r

dorth *loaf* 	**yn y bocs.** 
tuniau *tins*	**ar y silff.** 
bisgedi	**yn y cwpwrdd.**
menyn	**yn y cwpwrdd rhew.** *refrigerator.*

 DIOLCH YN FAWR IAWN.

If you're feeling exceptionally ambitious you can say what's inside each tin or frozen package as you hand it to your child.

Rho'r

ffa coch

cawl tomato

sbageti

 ar y silff, plîs.

Rho'r

pys

moron

blodfresych *cauliflower*

 yn y rhewgell, plîs. *freezer*

LLESTRI: GOSOD Y FORD
Dishes: Laying the Table

Useful Information

By the time that your child reaches 2½ you **may** *be able to hand him all the mats or (unbreakable) plates at once; say to him:*

Rho'r

matiau	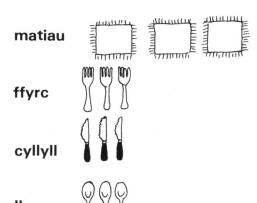
ffyrc	
cyllyll	
llwyau	
platiau	

**ar y ford,
os gweli di'n dda.**

and expect him to put them in the appropriate places.

Problem	Solution to the Problem
The normal arrangement of cutlery is much too difficult even for a three-year-old since it requires the concept of right and left.	1. *Have your child put all the cutlery together on each plate* **or** 2. *Make a set of model paper mats with the outline of forks, plates, knives, etc. drawn on them so that your child will know where each thing should go.*

Geirfa

llestri—*dishes*

lliain (bord) (m)—*tablecloth*
mat (m)—*mat*
  matiau—*mats*
napcyn (m)—*serviette*
  napcynau—*serviettes*

fforc (f)—*fork*
  ffyrc—*forks*

cyllell, y gyllell (f)—*knife*
  cyllyll—*knives*
llwy (f)—*spoon*
  llwyau—*spoons*
llwy de (f)—*teaspoon*

plât (m)—*plate*
  platiau—*plates*
dysgl, y ddysgl (f)—*bowl*
  dysglau—*bowls*

glás (m)—*glass*
  glasys—*glasses*

cwpan (m)—*cup*
  cwpanau—*cups*
soser (f)—*saucer*
  soseri—*saucers*

tebot (m)—*teapot*
basn siwgr (m)—*sugar bowl*
jwg (f)—*jug*

LLESTRI: GOLCHI'R LLESTRI
Dishes: Washing the Dishes

Bring: *a new and important command word*

Dere â'r
Bring the

tebot

basn siwgr

jwg

ddysgl

i fi, os gweli di'n dda.
to me, please.

Bring — **Dillad**

Dere â'r
Bring the

got

het

welis

menig

ymbarél

i Mami.

Bring — **Bwyd**

Dere â'r
Bring the

jam

afal

bisgedi

losin

creision

i fi.

Geirfa

cegin, y gegin (f)—*kitchen*

bord, y ford (f)—*table*
stôl (f)—*stool*
sinc (m)—*sink*
cwpwrdd (m)—*cupboard*
silff (f)—*shelf*
 (pronounced **shilff**)
 silffoedd—*shelves*
stof (f)—*cooker*
ffwrn (f)—*oven*
bwced sbwriel (m)—
 wastebin

peiriant golchi (m)—*washing machine*
sychydd (m)—*dryer*
cwpwrdd rhew (m)—
 refrigerator
rhewgell (f)—*freezer*
 (inside the refrigerator)
rhewgist (f)—*freezer*

tegell (m)—*kettle*
sosban (f)—*saucepan*
padell, y badell (f)—*large bowl*

padell ffrio, y badell ffrio (f)—
 frying pan
lliain (llestri) (m)—*tea towel*

dod—*to come*
 dere—*come (command—
 1 person, familiar)*
dod â—*to bring*
 dere â—*bring (command—
 1 person, familiar)*

Useful Information: *The ambitious parent can use the game to teach basic describing words too.*

'Wy'n cerdded
I'm walking

yn araf.
slowly.

yn gyflym.
quickly.

yn swnllyd.
noisily.

yn dawel.
quietly.

'Wy'n mynd
I'm becoming

yn fach.
small.

yn fawr.
big.

yn dew.
fat.

yn denau.
thin.

Notice *that in Welsh describing sentences the word* **yn/'n** *is necessary but can't be translated.*

Mae e'n hapus.
He is happy.

Mae hi'n cerdded yn hapus.
She is walking happily.

Maen nhw'n drist.
They are sad.

Describing Words

bach/yn fach—*little*
mawr/yn fawr—*big*
  ara'/yn ara'—*slow*
  cyflym/yn gyflym—*fast, quick*
tew/yn dew—*fat*
tenau/yn denau—*thin*
  swnllyd/yn swnllyd—*noisy*
  tawel/yn dawel—*quiet*
uchel/yn uchel—*high*
isel/yn isel—*low*
  hapus/yn hapus—*happy*
  trist/yn drist—*sad*

'Wy'n dawnsio'n
I'm dancing

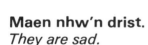

hapus.
happily.

drist.
sadly.

'Wy'n neidio'n uchel.
I'm jumping high.

'Wy'n plygu'n isel.
I'm bending low.

Action Words

cerdded—*to walk*
codi—*to get up, lift*
cropian—*to crawl*
chwarae—*to play*
chwerthin—*to laugh*
dawnsio—*to dance*
dringo—*to climb*

eistedd—*to sit*
gorwedd—*to lie (down)*
gwneud—*to make, do*
hedfan—*to fly*
hercian—*to hop*
llefain/crio—*to cry*
martsio—*to march*

mynd yn—*to become*
neidio—*to jump*
nofio—*to swim*
plygu—*to bend*
rhedeg—*to run*
sefyll—*to stand*
sgipio—*to skip*
troi—*to turn*

25
Y TYWYDD
The Weather

Cân y Tymhorau *(Song of the Seasons)*

Here is a song which will help you to teach the names and characteristics of three seasons to your child in Welsh. You make rising and falling motions with your hands (as appropriate) to the tune of "London Bridge is falling down".

Mae dail y coed yn cwympo i lawr
The leaves of the trees are falling down

Cwympo i lawr, cwympo i lawr.

Mae dail y coed yn cwympo i lawr

Yn yr hydre'.
In the autumn.

Mae eira gwyn yn cwympo i lawr
White snow is falling down

Cwympo i lawr, cwympo i lawr.

Mae eira gwyn yn cwympo i lawr

Yn y gaea'.
In the winter.

Mae blodau bach yn tyfu'n fawr
Little flowers are growing big

Tyfu'n fawr, tyfu'n fawr.

Mae blodau bach yn tyfu'n fawr

Yn y gwanwyn.
In the spring.

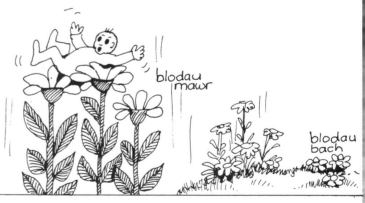

In the summer you can sing (to the tune of "Looby Loo")

Dyma ni, Lw-bi-lw.
Here we are, Looby Loo.

Dyma ni, Lw-bi-la.

Dyma ni, Lw-bi-lw.

Ar fore hyfryd o ha'.
On a lovely morning of summer.

Other Ways of Pointing Out Things In Town

Edrych ar
Look at

y plismon.

y gath.

yr awyren.

Wyt ti'n gweld
Do you see

yr ambiwlans?

y 'deryn?

y trên?

The Difference Between *OES* and *YDY*

Oes car yma?
Is a car here?

Oes.
Yes.

Ydy'r car yma?
Is the car here?

Ydy.
Yes.

Oes siop yma?
Is a siop here?

Nac oes.
No.

Ydy'r siop yma?
Is the shop here?

Nac ydy.
No.

Oes plant yno?
Are children there?

Oes.
Yes.

Ydy Mami yno?
Is Mammy there?

Ydy.
Yes.

Note:

1. **OES?** *(Is / Are?) is used in questions about general (non-specific) things (often preceded by "a").*

2. **YDY!** *(Is / Are?) is used in questions about people, when named, and specific things (preceded by "the").*

Useful Phrases

Paid â mynd ar yr heol.
Don't go on the road.

Aros ar y pafin.
Wait on the pavement.

Cydia yn fy llaw.
Take hold of my hand.

Dalia'n dynn.
Hold tightly.

Yn ofalus nawr.
Carefully now.

Geirfa

tre, y dre (f)—*town*
dinas, y ddinas (f)—*city*

menyw, y fenyw (f)—*woman*
  menywod—*women*
dyn (m)—*man*
  dynion—*men*
merch, y ferch (f)—*girl*
  merched—*girls*
bachgen (m)—*boy*
  bechgyn—*boys*
plismon (m)—*policeman*
dyn tân (m)—*fireman*

heol (f)—*street, road*

pafin (m)—*pavement*
to (m)—*roof*

siop (f)—*shop*
  siopau—*shops*
ysgol (f)—*school*
capel (m)—*chapel*
eglwys (f)—*church*
llyfrgell (f)—*library*
banc (m)—*banc*
sinema (f)—*cinema*
tafarn (m)—*pub*
caffi (m)—*cafe*
garej (f)—*garage*
ysbyty (m)—*hospital*

car (m)—*car*
bws (m)—*bus*
lori (f)—*lorry*
fan (f)—*van*
trên (m)—*train*
ambiwlans (m)—*ambulance*
injan dân (f)—*fire engine*
car heddlu (m)—*police car*
awyren (f)—*airplane*
hofrennydd (m)—*helicopter*

goleuadau—*traffic lights*

Useful Information

Y Geiriadur Lliwgar/ Welsh Children's Picture Dictionary *(Gwasg y Dref Wen, £3.95) is an especially handy book to use when you are naming things with your child. Children love it, and you'll find there the Welsh names of almost any person, animal, or thing that you are likely to encounter either inside or outside of the home.*

Still More Ways of Pointing Out Things

wiwer.

Dyna
There is / are
[*close by*]

'r bont.

oen bach.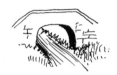

lori fawr.

gar Mr. Jones.

'deryn.

gastell.

'Co
There is / are
[*in the distance*]

'r môr.

'r fferm.

'r mynydd.

Geirfa

gwlad, y wlad (f)—*country*

wiwer (f)—*squirrel*
cwningen, y gwningen (f)—
 rabbit
oen (m)—*lamb*
 ŵyn—*lambs*
llo (m)—*calf*
 lloi—*calves*
pysgodyn (m)—*fish*
 pysgod—*fish(es)*
pili-pala (m)—*butterfly*

broga (m)—*frog*
crwban (m)—*tortoise*
neidr (f)—*snake*

mynydd (m)—*mountain*
 mynyddoedd—*mountains*
bryn (m)—*hill*
 bryniau—*hills*
cwm (m)—*valley*
 cymoedd—*valleys*
cae (m)—*field*
 caeau—*fields*
coedwig, y goedwig (f)—
 forest
môr (m)—*sea*
afon (f)—*river*
nant (f)—*stream*

ffordd (f)—*road*
pont, y bont (f)—*bridge*
fferm (f)—*farm*
ffermwr (m)—*farmer*
pentre (m)—*village*
castell (m)—*castle*

pert—*pretty*
 Mae'n bert.—*It's pretty.*
hardd—*beautiful*
 Mae'n hardd.—*It's
 beautiful.*
hyll—*ugly*
 Mae'n hyll.—*It's ugly.*

28
PERCHEN PETHAU
Owning Things

A Useful Variation

Beth sy 'da ni?
What do we have?

Mae
We've got

teledu

stof

hwnna

peiriant golchi,

cloc fel 'na
a clock like that

'da ni.*

*North Wales—gennyn ni

Useful Information

Mae hwn 'da* fi.—*I have this.* **
Mae hwn 'da ti.—*You have this.*
Mae hwn 'da fe.—*He has this.*
Mae hwn 'da hi.—*She has this.*

Mae hwnna 'da ni.—*We have that.*
Mae hwnna 'da chi.—*You have that.*
Mae hwnna 'da nhw.—*They have that.*
Mae hwnna 'da Dadi.—*Daddy has that.*

 * **'da = gyda** *(with)*
** *For North Wales forms see Supplement 2.*

The Negative Approach

Nac oes. Does dim
No. We don't have

sychydd
a dryer

beic modur
a motor-cycle

cloc mawr
a big clock

'da ni.

More Useful Information

You may also want to count things as you look at pictures in books and magazines.

Sawl bachgen sy yma?
How many boys are here?

Un dau.

Sawl 'deryn sy yma?
How many birds are here?

Un dau tri.

Sawl merch sy yma?
How many girls are here?

Un dwy tair.

Sawl un sy yma?
How many are here?

Un dau tri pedwar pump.

Notice that:

A. In English we say   **Yn Gymraeg**

How many boys?   *Sawl* **bachgen?**
Seven boys.   *Saith* **bachgen.**

How many girls?   *Sawl* **merch?**
Eight girls.   *Wyth* **merch.**

The **singular** *form of the noun is used after* **sawl** *and after numbers in Welsh.*

B. *The numbers 2, 3 and 4 have both masculine and feminine forms in Welsh.*

      dau/dwy   **tri/tair**   **pedwar/pedair**

When in doubt see the masculine form.

30
Y LLIWIAU/DISGRIFIO PETHAU
The Colours/Describing Things

Useful Information:	*The pictures below will give parents some practice with common describing words (and see p. 128).*

Mae'r tŷ'n fawr.
The house is big.

Ydy'r babi'n frwnt?   Ydy.
Is the baby dirty?   Yes.

Ydy'r plentyn yn ddrwg?   Nac ydy.
Is the child bad?   No.

Mawr/Bach

Tŷ

Da/Drwg

Plentyn

Tal/Byr/Hir

Dyn

Ci

Tew/Tenau

Menyw

Glân/Brwnt

Babi

Jam

Cas/Caredig

Bachgen

Hapus/Trist

Merch

Pert/Hyll

Tywysoges (Princess)   Gwrach (Witch)

You will notice that there are seven letters in Welsh (C, P, T, G, B, D, M—and also occasionally LL and RH) which change in certain circumstances.

C>G	G>—(dropped)	LL>L
P>B	B>F	M>F
T>D	D>DD	RH>R

Here are the three most important changes:

1) Feminine singular nouns after **y/'r**.

merch—y ferch   **cot—y got**   **dol—Ble mae'r ddol?**

2) Describing words after feminine singular nouns.

merch dda   **cot las**   **dol bert**

3) Describing words (adjectives or adverbs) after **yn**.

Mae'r bachgen yn drist.   **Mae e'n canu'n drist.**

IMPORTANT

Remembering what letters to change and which things are masculine and which feminine will come to you and your child with practice (singing songs, reading and hearing stories, etc.) and over a period of time.

Do not waste time and energy trying to memorize them!

Geirfa

tywysoges, y dywysoges (f)
  —princess
gwrach, y wrach (f)—witch

mawr—big
bach—little

da—good
drwg—bad

tal—tall
byr—short
hir—long

glân—clean
brwnt—dirty

cas—mean, nasty
caredig—kind

tew—fat
tenau—thin

pert—pretty
hardd—beautiful
hyll—ugly

hapus—happy
trist—sad

hen—old (comes before the
  thing it describes)
newydd—new

Hugan Goch Fach: Diwedd y stori *(The end of the story)*

Dyma Hugan Goch Fach. Mae hi'n bert.

Dyma Mr. Blaidd. Mae e'n hyll.

Dyma Mam-gu. Mae hi'n swnllyd.

Mae Mr. Blaidd yn gas.

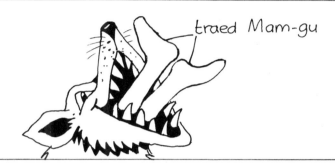

Mae Hugan Goch Fach yn garedig.

Mae dannedd Mr. Blaidd yn fawr.

Mae Mr. Blaidd yn ddrwg.

Mae Hugan Goch Fach yn drist.

Mae Dadi'n ddewr. *(brave)*

Mae'r deisen a'r llaeth yn dda.

Mae pawb *(everybody)* **yn hapus (ac yn dew).**

Supplement 1—Pronunciation

Learning to pronounce Welsh presents no problem at all to children and is easy even for their parents since in Welsh, unlike English, there is usually one sound only for each letter. You can master the essentials in a single session with your group leader or a Welsh speaking friend by reading aloud with them the words to the 10 songs at the beginning of the book. Your weekly practice sessions in the group should enable you to deal with any difficulties or uncertainties that occur thereafter.

A. Consonants

All consonants have one sound only in Welsh.

B	*as in*	**b**at
C	*as in*	**c**at
D	*as in*	**d**og
DD	*as in*	**th**e
F	*as in*	o**f**
FF	*as in*	o**ff**
G	*as in*	**g**o
NG	*as in*	so**ng**
H	*as in*	**h**at
J	*as in*	**j**am
L	*as in*	**l**et
LL	*as in*	**Ll**anelli
M	*as in*	**m**at
N	*as in*	**n**o
P	*as in*	**p**ot
PH	*as in*	**ph**otograph
R	*as in*	**r**at
RH	*as in*	**Rh**ys
S	*as in*	**s**at (but usually pronounced **sh** when followed by **i**, e.g. **siop** = shop)
T	*as in*	**t**op
TH	*as in*	**th**ink
W	*as in*	**w**ind

B. Vowels

The vowels in Welsh are : A E I O U W Y
They may be long or short.

	Long			Short		
A	tad *(father)*	as in	bard	mam *(mother)*	as in	ham
E	te *(tea)*	as in	mate	pen *(head)*	as in	then
			(as pronounced in S. Wales)			
I	fi *(I, me)*	as in	me	inc *(ink)*	as in	ink
O	bod *(to be)*	as in	more	cloc *(clock)*	as in	clock
U	un *(one)*	as in	keen	tun *(tin)*	as in	tin
W	cŵn *(dogs)*	as in	moon	lwc *(luck)*	as in	look
Y	dyn *(man)*	as in	keen	mynd *(to go)*	as in	tin

Y also has the sound heard in the English **fun.**

This occurs in:

1. **y** *(the)*   **yr** *(the)*   **yn** *(in)*   **fy** *(my)*   **dy** *(your)*

2. *Any syllable* **but** *the final one in words of more than one syllable.*

         cysgu *(to sleep)*   **gyrru** *(to drive)*   **bysedd** *(fingers)*

Note

In spoken Welsh a vowel is inserted between two consonants in a final syllable.

     llyfr *(book)*—**llyfyr**   **gafr** *(goat)*—**gafar**   **pobl** *(people)*—**pobol**

You will notice that the inserted vowel is usually the same as the one in the preceding syllable.

C. Dipthongs

AI AE AU	as in	aye/I	**Paid!** (Don't!) **cae** (field) **cau** (shut)

Note:
When AI and AU come at the end of a word they are pronounced **eh** (but **ah** in certain part of North Wales).

llyfrau (books)>**llyfreh** **cadair** (chair)>**cadehr**	**ceffylau** (horses)>**ceffyleh** **pedair** (four)>**pedehr**

AW	as in	ah-oo	**pawb** (everybody)

EI EU EY	as in	may	**cei** (quay) **teulu** (family) **meysedd** (meadows)

Note:
EI (his / her) and EU (their) are both pronounced **ee**.

EW	as in	the **e** of **ten** followed by **w** (as in **look**)	**newydd** (new)
IW UW YW	as in	new/queue	**lliw** (colour) **Duw** (God) **yw** (is)
OE OI OU	as in	boy	**oed** (age) **cloi** (to lock) **cyffrous** (exciting)
OW	as in	brown	**brown** (brown)
IA	as in	yap	**iawn** (very)
IE	as in	yes	**Iesu** (Jesus)
WY	as in as in	window oo-ee	**gwyn** (white) **bwyd** (food)

D. Stress

In Welsh the stress normally falls on the last syllable but one.

plentyn (child)	**athr**awes (teacher)	**bore** (morning)

Supplement 2—North and South *(differences in vocabulary and pronunciation)*

	De Cymru / *South Wales*	Gogledd Cymru / *North Wales*
1.	**dihuno**	**deffro**—*to wake up*
2.	**Shwd 'wyt ti?** **heddi'** **cusan**	**Sut wyt ti**—*How are you? (one person familiar)* **heddiw**—*today* **sws (m)**—*kiss*
p. 12	**dere** **Ishte lawr.**	**tyrd**—*come (command—one person, familiar)* **Eistedda.**—*Sit down. (command—one person, familiar)*

3.	**menyw**
	
	merch
	
	eisiau *(pronounced* **eesheh***)*
		dynes, y ddynes (f)—*woman*
		  gwragedd—*women*
		geneth, yr eneth (f)—*girl*
		  genethod—*girls*
		eisiau *(pronounced* **eesho***)*—*to want*

4.	**bola**	**bol (m)**—*stomach*
5.	**da**	**gwartheg**—*cattle*
6.	**nawr** **lliain** **brwnt**	**rŵan**—*now* **tywel (m)**—*towel* **budr**—*dirty*

7.	**pants**
	trowsus
	e / fe
	'wy / rwy
	cer / cere
	ffedog
	gwisg nos
	clwt
	
	neisied
		trôns (m)—*underpants*
		trwsus (m)—*trousers*
		o / fo—*he, him*
		'dwi / rydw i—*I am*
		dos—*go (command—one person, familiar)*
		brat (m)—*apron*
		coban, y goban (f)—*nightgown*
		cadach (m)—*nappy*
		  cadachau—*nappies*
		hances (m)—*handkerchief*
		  hancesi—*handkerchiefs*

8.	**llaeth** **dysgl** **b'yta** **wy**	**llefrith (m)**—*milk* **powlen, y bowlen (f)**—*bowl* **bwyta**—*to eat* **wŷ (m)**—*egg*
p. 29	**corryn** **malwoden**	**pry copyn (m)**—*spider* **malwen, y falwen (f)**—*snail*
9.	**cawl** **bara menyn** **losin** **twym** **twym iawn**	**potes (m)**—*soup* **brechdan, y frechdan (f)**—*slice of buttered bread* **fferins / da-da / pethau da**—*sweets* **cynnes**—*warm* **poeth**—*hot*

134

	De Cymru / *South Wales*	Gogledd Cymru / *North Wales*

10.	rhagor
	ffowlyn
	winwns
	peren
	
	tarten
	teisen
		(y)chwaneg—*more*
		cyw iâr (m)—*chicken*
		nionod—*onions*
		gellygen, yr ellygen (f)—*pear*
		   gellyg—*pears*
		pastai, y bastai (f)—*tart*
		cacen, y gacen (f)—*cake*
		   cacennau—*cakes*

p. 34	bord	bwrdd (m)—*table*
11.	pen-lin gwddwg	pen-glin (m)—*knee* gwddw (m)—*neck, throat*
12.	ma's	allan—*out*
13.	yw	ydy—*is / are*
14.	mam-gu tad-cu siten	nain (f)—*grandmother* taid (m)—*grandfather* cynfas (m)—*sheet* cynfasau—*sheets*
15.	celfi 'stafell wely cornel (m)	dodrefn—*furniture* llofft (f)—*bedroom* cornel, y gornel (f)—*corner*
17.	whilber Rho _____ heibio.	berfa, y ferfa (f)—*wheelbarrow* Rho _____ i gadw.—*Put _____ away.*
p. 58	Mae'n flin 'da fi.	Mae'n ddrwg gen i.—*I'm sorry.*
p. 59	simnai perth clwyd	simdde (f)—*chimney* gwrych (m)—*hedge* llidiart (m)—*gate* gât (f)—*gate*
18.	stâr cwts dan stâr	grisiau—*stairs* twll dan y grisiau (m)—*cupboard under the stairs*
19.	dod	dŵad—*to come*
20.	gwair mwydyn cwympo lan 'Sdim ots. llefain	glaswellt (m)—*grass* pry genwair (m)—*worm* syrthio—*to fall* i fyny—*up* Hidia befo.—*It doesn't matter.* crio—*to cry*
21.	gyda	efo—*with*

	De Cymru/ *South Wales*	**Gogledd Cymru**/ *North Wales*
22.	cwpan (m)	cwpan, y gwpan (f) — *cup*
23.	ffwrn dere â	popty (m) — *oven* tyrd â — *bring (command — one person, familiar)*
26.	heol	ffordd (f) — *road, street* lon (f) — *lane, street*
27.	'co pert	dacw — *there is / are (in the distance)* tlws — *pretty*

28.	Mae het 'da Nia.
	
	Mae het 'da fi, ti, fe, hi,
	
	      'da ni, chi, nhw.
		Mae het gan Nia. — *Nia has a hat.*
		  (Literally — A hat is with Nia.)
		Mae het gen i, gen ti / gennyt ti, ganddo fe,
		  ganddi hi,
		  gennyn ni / gynnon ni, gennych chi / gynnoch
		  chi, ganddyn nhw. — *I, You (etc.) have a hat.*

30.	caredig	clên — *kind, agreeable*

Supplement 3—Cymraeg Trwy'r Dydd (Welsh Through the Day)

1.	AMSER CODI *(Time to get up)*	

A.	**Cyfarchion**	*Greetings*
	Bore da, cariad.	*Good morning, love.*
	Mae'n amser codi.	*It's time to get up.*
	Mae'n bwrw glaw / Mae'n braf heddi'.	*It's raining / It's fine today.*
	Mae'n oer / Mae'n gymylog y bore 'ma.	*It's cold / It's cloudy this morning.*

B.	**Mynd i'r tŷ bach**	*Going to the toilet*
	Cer i'r tŷ bach nawr.	*Go to the toilet now.*
	Yn gyflym, gyflym.	*Quickly, quickly.*

C.	**Ymolchi**	*Washing*
	Golcha dy wyneb. / dy ddwylo.	*Wash your face. / your hands.*
	Sycha dy wyneb / dy ddwylo nawr.	*Dry your face / your hands now.*
	Brwsia dy ddannedd.	*Brush your teeth.*
	Dyma'r clwtyn. / lliain. / sebon.	*Here's the facecloth. / towel. / soap.*
	Cân: **Dyma'r ffordd i olchi wyneb**	**Song:** *This is the way to wash (your) face*

D.	**Gwisgo**	*Dressing*
	Ble mae dy bants? / dy fest? / etc.	*Where are your pants? / your vest? / etc.*
	Dyma dy bants. / dy fest. / etc.	*Here are your pants. / your vest. / etc.*
	Cer i ôl dy bants. / dy fest. / etc.	*Go to fetch your pants. / your fest. / etc.*
	Gwisga dy bants. / dy fest. / etc.	*Put on your pants. / your vest. / etc.*
	Brwsia dy wallt nawr.	*Brush your hair now.*
	Gêm: **Ble mae Dewi? / Nia?**	**Game:** *Where's Dewi? / Nia? (as you pull jumper, etc. over child's head)*
	Dyma fe! / Dyma hi!	*Here he is! / Here she is!*
	Cân: **Fel hyn 'wy'n gwisgo 'sanau, etc.**	**Song:** *Like this I put on socks, etc.*

2.	AMSER BRECWAST / CINIO / TE / SWPER	

A.	**Gosod y ford**	*Laying the table*
	Cwpan (etc.) i Mami. / i Dadi. / i ti.	*A cup (etc.) for Mammy. / for Daddy. / for you.*
	Rho'r _____ ar y ford.	*Put the _____ on the table.*
	Cân: **Rhowch y lliain ar y ford**	**Song:** *Put the cloth on the table*

B.	**Cael bwyd**	*Having food*
	Dyma'r _____.	*Here's the _____.*
	Wyt ti eisiau _____? Ydw. / Nac ydw.	*Do you want _____? Yes. / No.*
	Estyn y _____ i fi.	*Pass the _____ to me.*
	Cân: **Fel hyn 'wy'n b'yta / yfed _____**	**Song:** *Like this I eat / drink _____*

C.	Golchi'r llestri	Washing the dishes
	Rho'r _____ i fi.	Give the _____ to me.
	Rho'r _____ yn y dŵr.	Put the _____ in the water.
	Dere â'r _____ i fi.	Bring the _____ to me.
	Golcha'r _____./Sycha'r _____.	Wash the _____. / Dry the _____.
	Cân: Oes cwpan yn y dŵr?	**Song:** *Is (there) a cup in the water?*

3.	**GOLCHI DWYLO/TŶ BACH** *(Washing Hands / Toilet)*	
	Mae'n amser golchi/sychu dwylo.	*It's time to wash / dry (your) hands.*
	Cer i olchi/sychu dwylo nawr.	*Go to wash / dry (your) hands now.*
	Wyt ti eisiau mynd i'r tŷ bach?	*Do you want to go to the toilet? Yes. / No.*
	Ydw. / Na.	

4.	**GOLCHI DILLAD** *(Washing Clothes)*	
A.	**Rhoi'r dillad yn y peiriant/ y sychydd**	*Putting the clothes in the machine / the dryer*
	Sgert Mami./Pants Nia./etc.	*Mammy's skirt. / Nia's pants. / etc.*
	Rho _____ i mewn.	*Put _____ in.*
B.	**Rhoi'r dillad ar y lein**	*Putting the clothes on the line*
	Ble mae crys Dadi?/fest Nia?/etc.	*Where's Daddy's shirt? / Nia's vest? / etc.*
	Rho grys Dadi/fest Nia, etc. i fi.	*Give Daddy's shirt / Nia's vest, etc. to me.*
C.	**Dosbarthu'r dillad**	*Sorting the clothes*
	Ble mae 'sanau Dewi?/blows Mami?/etc.	*Where are Dewi's socks? / Mammy's blouse? / etc.*

5.	**CHWARAE** *(Playing)*	
A.	**Paratoi**	*Preparing*
	Cer i ôl _____.	*Go to fetch _____.*
	Mae e yn/ar/dan/wrth/tu ôl i _____.	*It's in / on / under / by / behind _____.*
B.	**Gemau**	*Games*
	Cuddio, Follow the leader, Mr. Blaidd, etc.	*Hide and Seek, Follow the leader, Mr. Wolf, etc.*
C.	**Gwaith celf**	*Art work*
	Dyma'r papur./paent coch./etc.	*Here's the paper. / red paint. / etc.*
	Wyt ti eisiau'r creon glas?/etc. Ydw. / Nac ydw.	*Do you want the blue crayon?/etc. Yes. / No.*
D.	**Tacluso**	*Tidying up*
	Rho _____ yn y bocs./etc.	*Put _____ in the box. / etc.*
	Rho _____ heibio.	*Put _____ away.*

6.	**CANU /DARLLEN** *(Singing / Reading)*	

	(At least once a day for at least 10 minutes at a time)	
	Dyma _____./Dyna _____.	*Here is / are _____. / There is / are _____.*
	Ble mae _____? Fan hyn./Fanna.	*Where is / are _____? Here. / There.*
	Pwy yw hwn?/ hon?	*Who is this? (masc. / fem.)*
	Beth yw hwn?/ hwnna?	*What is this? / that?*
	Pwy / Beth sy yna?	*Who / What is there?*
	Beth mae e'n (ei) wneud?	*What is he doing?*
	Beth mae e'n (ei) ddweud?	*What does he say?*

7.	**MYND MA'S** *(Going out)*	

A.	**Gwisgo**	*Dressing*
	Cer i ôl dy got/het./etc. nawr.	*Go to fetch your coat / hat / etc. now.*
	Mae e yn y cwpwrdd, etc.	*It's in the cupboard, etc.*
	Gwisga dy got, etc. nawr.	*Put on your coat, etc. now.*
B.	**Yn y dre, etc.**	*In town, etc.*
	Name anything that you can in Welsh	
	Dyma'r afon./y bws./siop Mr. Owen.	*Here's the river. / the bus. / Mr. Owen's shop.*
	Oes lori, etc. yma? Oes. / Nac oes.	*Is (there) a lorry, etc. here? Yes. / No.*
	Edrych ar y ci./yr ambiwlans./etc.	*Look at the dog. / the ambulance. / etc.*
	Wyt ti'n gweld y defaid?/y môr?	*Do you see the sheep? / the sea?*
C.	**Tynnu dillad**	*Undressing*
	Tynna dy got./dy welis./etc.	*Take off your coat. / your wellies. / etc.*
	Rho nhw yn y cwpwrdd, etc.	*Put them in the cupboard, etc.*

8.	**AMSER GWELY** *(Bedtime)*	

A.	**Tynnu dillad**	*Undressing*
	Tynna dy 'sanau./dy grys./etc.	*Take off your socks. / your shirt. / etc.*
	Rho fe yn y drôr./ar y gadair./etc.	*Put it in the drawer. / on the chair. / etc.*
	Cân: **Fel hyn 'wy'n tynnu 'sgidiau, etc.**	*Song: Like this I take off shoes, etc.*
B.	**Cael bath**	*Having a bath*
	Dyma'r sebon./sbwng./etc.	*Here's the soap. / sponge. / etc.*
	Wyt ti eisiau'r cwch, etc. heno?	*Do you want the boat, etc. tonight?*
	Ydw. / Nac ydw.	*Yes. / No.*
	Ble mae dy gefn, etc.? Fan hyn!	*Where's your back, etc? Here!*
	Cân: **Dyma'r ffordd i olchi coesau, etc.**	*Song: This is the way to wash (your) leg, etc.*
C.	**Darllen/ Canu**	*Reading / Singing*
	(See above)	
D.	**Dweud ''Nos da''**	*Saying ''Goodnight''*
	Mae'n amser cysgu nawr.	*It's time to sleep now.*
	Rho gusan i fi.	*Give me a kiss.*
	Nos da, cariad.	*Goodnight, love.*

Supplement 4

Detachable Vocabulary Sheets
(to be fastened to the appropriate wall when necessary)

1
Y CORFF
The Body

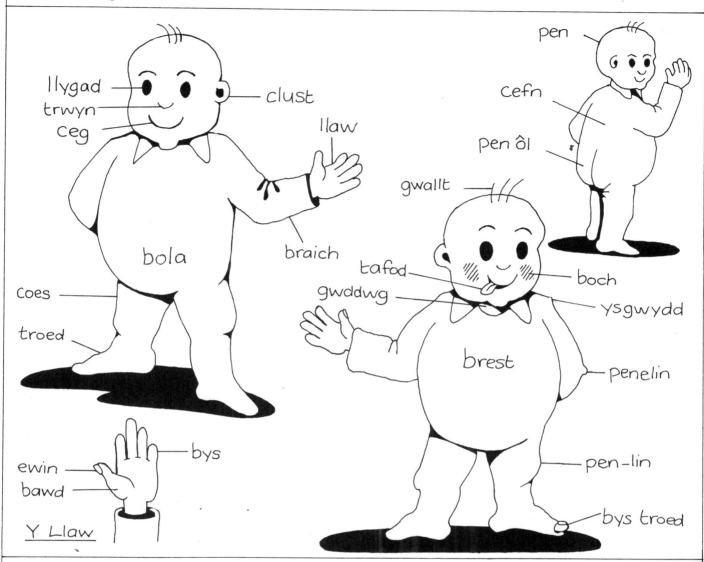

llygad
trwyn
ceg
clust
llaw
bola
braich
coes
troed
ewin
bawd
bys
Y Llaw

pen
cefn
pen ôl
gwallt
tafod
gwddwg
boch
ysgwydd
brest
penelin
pen-lin
bys troed

Geirfa

pen (m) — *head*
llygad (f) — *eye*
  llygaid — *eyes*
clust, y glust (f) — *ear*
  clustiau — *ears*
trwyn (m) — *nose*
ceg, y geg (f) — *mouth*

gwallt (m) — *hair*
wyneb (m) — *face*
talcen (m) — *forehead*
boch, y foch (f) — *cheek*
  bochau — *cheeks*
gwefus, y wefus (f) — *lip*
  gwefusau — *lips*
dant (m) — *tooth*
  dannedd — *teeth*

tafod (m) — *tongue*

gwddwg (m) — *neck, throat*
ysgwydd (f) — *shoulder*
  ysgwyddau — *shoulders*
brest, y frest (f) — *chest*
bola (m) — *stomach*

braich, y fraich (f) — *arm*
  breichiau — *arms*
penelin (m) — *elbow*
llaw (f) — *hand*
  dwylo — *hands*
bys (m) — *finger*
  bysedd — *fingers*
bawd (m) — *thumb*

ewin (m) — *fingernail*
  ewinedd — *fingernails*

cefn (m) — *back*
pen ôl (m) — *bottom*

coes, y goes (f) — *leg*
  coesau — *legs*
pen-lin, y ben-lin (f) — *knee*
  penliniau — *knees*
troed, y droed (f) — *foot*
  traed — *feet*
bys troed (m) — *toe*
  bysedd traed — *toes*
bys dy droed — *your toe*
  bysedd dy draed — *your toes*

2
DILLAD
Clothes

Merch *(Girl)*	Bachgen *(Boy)*

Pants

Fest

Pais

Ffrog

Cardigan

'Sanau

'Sgidiau

Pants

Fest

Crys

Trowsus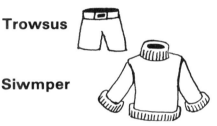

Siwmper

'Sanau

'Sgidiau

Geirfa

dillad—*clothes*

pants (m)—*underpants*
fest (f)—*vest*
pais, y bais (f)—*petticoat*

ffrog (f)—*dress*
sgert (f)—*skirt*
blows, y flows (f)—*blouse*
ffedog (f)—*apron*
cardigan, y gardigan (f)—
   cardigan

crys (m)—*shirt*
trowsus (m)—*trousers*
trowsus byr (m)—*shorts*
tei (m)—*tie*
siwmper (f)—*jumper*
siaced (f)—*jacket*

teits (m)—*tights*
hosan (f)—*sock, stockings*
   'sanau—*socks, stockings*
   (pronounced **saneh***)*
esgid (f)—*shoe*
   'sgidiau—*shoes*
   (pronounced **sgidieh***)*

dillad nos—*pyjamas*
gwisg nos, y wisg nos (f)—
   nightgown
sliper (f)—*slipper*
   sliperi—*slippers*

clwt (m)—*nappy*
   clytiau—*nappies*

neisied (f)—*handkerchief*
   neisiedon—*handkerchiefs*

cot, y got (f)—*coat*
cot law, y got law (f)—
   raincoat
het (f)—*hat*
cap (m)—*cap*
maneg, y faneg (f)—*glove*
   menig—*gloves*
sgarff (f)—*scarf*
ymbarél (m)—*umbrella*

gwisgo—*to put on, wear*
tynnu—*to take off, pull*

Note: *Notice that the clothes most obviously belonging to a boy are masculine and that practically everything else is feminine.*

3
BWYD BRECWAST
Breakfast Food

Sudd Oren	Uwd *Porridge*	Creision Ŷd *Cornflakes*

Sudd Oren: jwg, glás, oren

Uwd: basn siwgr, llaeth, uwd

Creision Ŷd: Creision Ŷd, dysgl, llwy

Tost	Wy	Llaeth / Coffi / Te

Tost: mêl, tost, menyn

Wy: wy (wedi ferwi), llwy, wy (wedi ffrio), cig moch *bacon*, bara saim *fried bread*

Llaeth / Coffi / Te: llaeth, te, llwy de, coffi heb siwgr *coffee without sugar*

Geirfa

bwyd (m) — *food*
brecwast (m) — *breakfast*

sudd oren (m) — *orange juice*
uwd (m) — *porridge*
creision ŷd — *corn flakes*
sirial (m) — *cereal*

tost (m) — *toast*
menyn (m) — *butter*

marmalêd (m) — *marmalade*
jam (m) — *jam*
mêl (m) — *honey*

cig moch (m) — *bacon*
bara saim (m) — *fried bread*
wy (m) — *egg*
wy wedi (ei) ferwi — *boiled egg*
wy wedi (ei) ffrio — *fried egg*
wy wedi (ei) falu — *scrambled egg*

wy wedi (ei) botsio — *poached egg*

llaeth (m) — *milk*
te (m) — *tea*
coffi (m) — *coffee*
siwgr (m) — *sugar*

bwyta — *to eat (pronounced b'yta in S. Wales)*
yfed — *to drink*

4
BWYD CINIO
Dinner Food

Cawl	**Sosej / Ffa Coch / Wy** *Baked Beans*	**Brechdanau** *Sandwiches*
 bara menyn cawl llwy	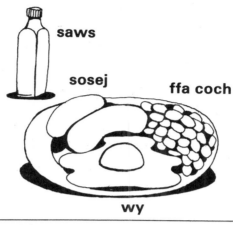 saws sosej ffa coch wy	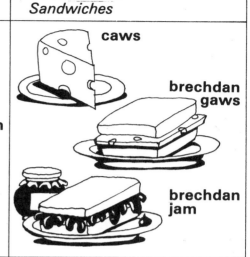 caws brechdan gaws brechdan jam
Pysgod a Sglodion *Fish and Chips*	**Ffrwythau** *Fruit*	**Bisgedi a Losin** *Biscuits and Sweets*
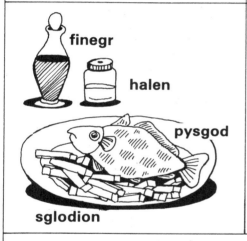 finegr halen pysgod sglodion	 afal oren banana	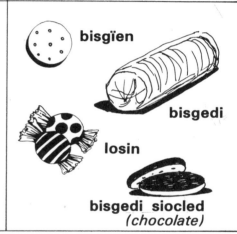 bisgïen bisgedi losin bisgedi siocled *(chocolate)*

Geirfa

cinio (m) — *dinner*

cawl (m) — *soup*
wy (m) — *egg*
  wyau — *eggs*
sosej (f) — *sausage*
selsig (f) — *sausage*
pastai, y bastai (f) — *pie, pasty*
pysgodyn (m) — *fish (one)*
  pysgod — *fish(es)*

pys — *peas*
ffa coch — *baked beans*
sbageti — *spaghetti*
tatws — *potatoes*
  taten, y daten (f) — *potato*

sglodion / sglods / tsips — *chips*

bara (m) — *bread*
torth, y dorth (f) — *loaf*
  torth wen — *white loaf*
  torth frown — *brown loaf*
bara menyn (m) — *bread and butter*
brechdan, y frechdan (f) — *sandwich*
  brechdanau — *sandwiches*
caws (m) — *cheese*

finegr (m) — *vinegar*
saws (m) — *sauce*
pupur (m) — *pepper*
halen (m) — *salt*

afal (m) — *apple*
  afalau — *apples*
banana (m) — *banana*
  bananas — *bananas*
oren (m) — *orange*
  orennau — *oranges*

creision — *crisps*
bisgïen, y fisgïen (f) — *biscuit*
  bisgedi — *biscuits*
losin — *sweets*
siocled (m) — *chocolate*

diod, y ddiod (f) — *drink*
dŵr (m) — *water*
pop (m) — *pop*

5
BWYD TE / SWPER
Tea / Supper Food

Cig / Pys / Tatws *Meat / Peas / Potatoes*	Ffowlyn / Grefi *Chicken / Gravy*	Llysiau *Vegetables*

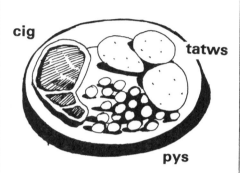

cig
tatws
pys

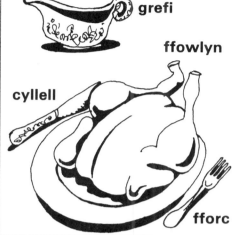

grefi
ffowlyn
cyllell
fforc

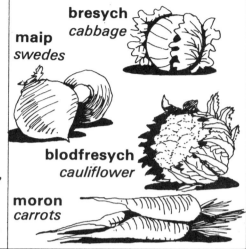

bresych *cabbage*
maip *swedes*
blodfresych *cauliflower*
moron *carrots*

Salad	Teisennau *Cakes*	Pwdin

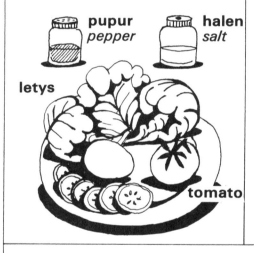

pupur *pepper*
halen *salt*
letys
tomato

teisennau
teisen jam *jam cake*

pwdin reis *rice pudding*

hufen iâ *ice cream*

Geirfa

te (m) — *tea*
swper (m) — *supper*

cig (m) — *meat*
cig eidion (m) — *beef*
cig oen (m) — *lamb*
cig llo (m) — *veal*
porc (m) — *pork*
ham (m) — *ham*
stêc (m) — *steak*
ffowlyn (m) — *chicken*
grefi (m) — *gravy*

llysiau — *vegetables*
moron — *carrots*
bresych — *cabbage*

blodfresych — *cauliflower*
winwns — *onions*
madarch — *mushrooms*
maip — *swedes*
pannas — *parsnips*
letys — *lettuce*
tomato (m) — *tomato*
cucumer (m) — *cucumber*
salad (m) — *salad*
reis (m) — *rice*

ffrwythau — *fruit*
peren, y beren (f) — *pear*
  pêr — *pears*
grawnwin — *grapes*
metus — *strawberries*

eirinen (f) — *plum*
  eirin — *plums*
cnau — *nuts*

pwdin (m) — *pudding*
pwdin reis (m) — *rice pudding*
hufen iâ (m) — *ice cream*
tarten, y darten (f) — *tart*
  tarten afalau — *apple tart*
  tarten riwbob — *rhubarb tart*
  tarten fwyar duon — *blackberry tart*
cwstard (m) — *custard*
teisen, y deisen (f) — *cake*
  teisennau — *cakes*

6
LLESTRI
Dishes

jwg

tebot

basn siwgr

glás

cwpan

soser

llwy

llwy de

fforc

plât

cyllell

Geirfa

llestri — *dishes*

lliain (bord) (m) — *tablecloth*
mat (m) — *mat*
  matiau — *mats*
napcyn (m) — *serviette*
  napcynau — *serviettes*

fforc (f) — *fork*
  ffyrc — *forks*

cyllell, y gyllell (f) — *knife*
  cyllyll — *knives*
llwy (f) — *spoon*
  llwyau — *spoons*
llwy de (f) — *teaspoon*

plât (m) — *plate*
  platiau — *plates*
dysgl, y ddysgl (f) — *bowl*
  dysglau — *bowls*

glás (m) — *glas*
  glasys — *glasses*

cwpan (m) — *cup*
  cwpanau — *cups*
soser (f) — *saucer*
  soseri — *saucers*

tebot (m) — *teapot*
basn siwgr (m) — *sugar bowl*
jwg (f) — *jug*

7
TEGANAU
Toys

pêl	dol	tedi	tŷ dol

car	trên	lori	ambiwlans

llestri te	llyfr	blociau	jig-so

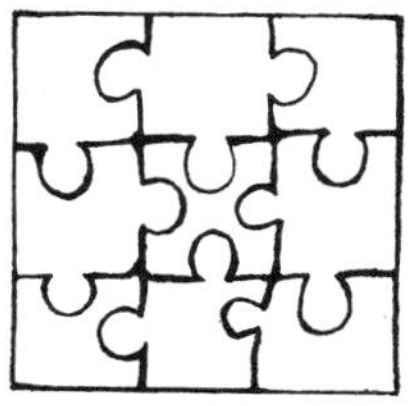

llestri te labels: basn siwgr, plât, tebot, cwpan, soser, jwg

blociau labels: A B C FF E D

awyren	beic	ceffyl pren	whilber

Geirfa

tegan (m) — *toy*
  teganau — *toys*

tedi (m) — *teddy*
dol / doli, y ddol / ddoli (f) —
  doll
pêl, y bêl (f) — *ball*
  peli — *balls*
llyfr (m) — *book (pronounced*
  llyfyr)
  llyfrau — *books*
bloc (m) — *block*
  blociau — *blocks*

gêm (f) — *game*
  gemau — *games*
jig-so (m) — *jigsaw puzzle*

beic (m) — *bicycle*
ceffyl pren (m) — *rocking*
  (literally: wooden) horse
whilber (f) — *wheelbarrow*

tŷ dol (m) — *doll's house*
llestri te — *teaset (literally:*
  tea dishes)

car (m) — *car*
  ceir — *cars*
lori (f) — *lorry*
  loriau — *lorries*
trên (m) — *train*
ambiwlans (m) — *ambulance*
awyren (f) — *airplane*
  awyrennau — *airplanes*
llong (f) — *ship*
  llongau — *ships*

155

8

Y 'STAFELL 'MOLCHI
The Bathroom

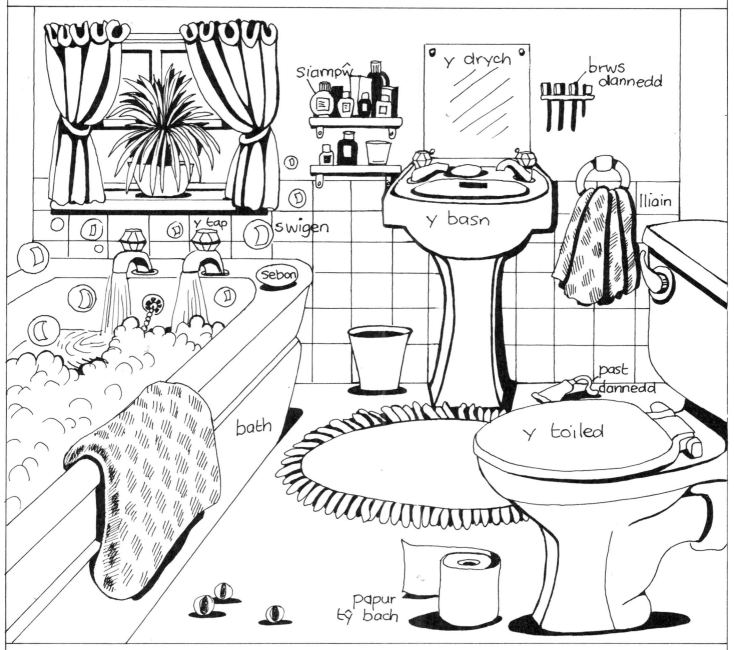

siampŵ
y drych
brws dannedd
swigen
y tap
y basn
lliain
sebon
bath
past dannedd
y toiled
papur tŷ bach

Geirfa

bath (m) — *bath, bathtub*
basn (ymolchi) (m) — *washbasin*
cawod, y gawod (f) — *shower*
tŷ bach (m) — *lavatory*
toiled (m) — *toilet*
drych (m) — *mirror*

lliain (m) — *towel*
  llieiniau — *towels*
clwtyn (m) — *facecloth*
  clytiau — *facecloths*
sbwng (m) — *sponge*

gwlanen, y wlanen (f) — *flannel*

dŵr (m) — *water*
sebon (m) — *soap*
siampŵ (m) — *shampoo*
swigen (m) — *bubble*
  swigod — *bubbles*
brws dannedd (m) — *toothbrush*
past dannedd (m) — *toothpaste*

papur tŷ bach (m) — *toilet paper*

oer — *cold*
twym — *warm*
twym iawn — *hot*
brwnt — *dirty*
glân — *clean*
glwyb — *wet*
sych — *dry*

golchi — *to wash*
sychu — *to dry*
brwsio — *to brush*

9
Y 'STAFELL WELY
The Bedroom

llenni

golau

drws

pêl

ffenest

llun

cwpwrdd

gobennydd

gwely

stôl

dol

llyfrau

lamp

bord

cadair

llyfr

tedi

llygoden

Geirfa

gwely (m) — *bed*
cadair, y gadair (f) — *chair*
bord, y ford (f) — *table*
cwpwrdd (m) — *cupboard*
desg, y ddesg (f) — *desk*
biwrô (m) — *bureau*
drôr (m) — *drawer*

llun (m) — *picture*
  lluniau — *pictures*
silff (f) — *shelf (pronounced*
  shilff *in S. Wales)*
silff lyfrau (f) — *bookshelf*
silffoedd llyfrau — *bookcase*
gobennydd (m) — *pillow*

drws (m) — *door*
ffenest (f) — *window*
llawr (m) — *floor*
carped (m) — *carpet*
wal (f) — *wall*
  waliau — *walls*
cornel (m) — *corner*
nenfwd (f) — *ceiling*
golau (m) — *light*

10

Y 'STAFELL FYW
The Living Room

Geirfa

celfi — *furniture*

soffa (f) — *sofa*
clustog, y glustog (f) — *pillow, cushion*
  clustogau — *pillows, cushions*
cadair, y gadair (f) — *chair*
  cadeiriau — *chairs*
bord, y ford (f) — *table*
  bordydd — *tables*

llen (f) — *curtain*
  llenni — *curtains*

carped (m) — *carpet*

tân (m) — *fire*
lle tân (m) — *fireplace*
silff ben tân (f) — *mantelpiece*

llun (m) — *picture*
  lluniau — *pictures*
piano (m) — *piano*
silff lyfrau (f) — *bookshelf*
silffoedd llyfrau — *bookcase*

telyn, y delyn (f) — *harp*
teledu (m) — *television set*

cloc (m) — *clock*
lamp (f) — *lamp*
golau (m) — *light*
  goleuadau — *lights*

ffenest (f) — *window*
  ffenestri — *windows*
drws (m) — *door*

11
Y GEGIN
The Kitchen

- ffenest
- cloc
- padell ffrio
- cwpwrdd
- stof
- silff
- tegell
- sosban fach
- sosban fawr
- llestri
- tap
- Sinc
- ffwrn
- cwpwrdd rhew
- peiriant golchi
- jwg
- padell
- bwced sbwriel
- cath
- llwy
- bord
- stôl

Geirfa

cegin, y gegin (f) — *kitchen*

bord, y ford (f) — *table*
stôl (f) — *stool*
sinc (m) — *sink*
cwpwrdd (m) — *cupboard*
silff (f) — *shelf (pronounced
  shilff)*
  silffoedd — *shelves*
stof (f) — *cooker*

ffwrn (f) — *oven*
bwced sbwriel (m) —
  wastebin
peiriant golchi (m) — *washing
  machine*
sychydd (m) — *dryer*
cwpwrdd rhew (m) —
  refrigerator
rhewgell (f) — *freezer (inside
  the refrigerator)*

rhewgist (f) — *freezer*

tegell (m) — *kettle*
sosban (f) — *saucepan*
padell, y badell (f) — *large
  bowl*
padell ffrio, y badell ffrio (f) —
  frying pan
lliain (llestri) (m) — *tea towel*